Re-thinking Children's Work in Churches

RE-THINKING CHILDREN'S WORK IN CHURCHES

A Practical Guide

Edited by CAROLYN EDWARDS,
SIAN HANCOCK and SALLY NASH

Jessica Kingsley *Publishers*
London and Philadelphia

First published in 2019
by Jessica Kingsley Publishers
73 Collier Street
London N1 9BE, UK
and
400 Market Street, Suite 400
Philadelphia, PA 19106, USA

www.jkp.com

Library of Congress Cataloging in Publication Data
A CIP catalog record for this book is available from the Library of Congress

British Library Cataloguing in Publication Data
A CIP catalogue record for this book is available from the British Library

ISBN 978 1 78592 125 4
eISBN 978 1 78450 389 5

Printed and bound in Great Britain

This book is dedicated to all of those who are involved in ministry with children and who have invested so much as witnesses and proclaimers of the Gospel alongside children inside and outside of the Church. Thank you for the difference you make in their lives.

Acknowledgements

Thanks to all of our authors for their commitment to this project and to Natalie Watson, our editor at Jessica Kingsley Publishers, for her enthusiasm to make this book happen.

Contents

Introduction: All of God's Children   9
Sally Nash, Founding Director of the Midlands Institute for Children, Youth and Mission (MCYM), Associate Priest, Hodge Hill Church, Birmingham, and researcher, Centre for Paediatric Spiritual Care, Birmingham Women's and Children's Hospital

1. Train Driver: Growing through Experience   18
Isobel MacDougall, parent support worker

2. Teddy Bear: Holding the Whispers Shared in the Dark   33
Paul Nash, Chaplaincy and Spiritual Care Team Leader, Birmingham Women's and Children's Hospital, and tutor, Midlands Institute for Children, Youth and Mission

3. Facebook Friend: Socialisation, Socialising and Social Networking   53
Carolyn Edwards, Children and Youth Adviser, Diocese of York

4. Gracious Grandparent: Working with Families   64
Martyn Payne, formerly of the Bible Reading Fellowship and a Messy Church researcher

5. Clown and Fool: Fun and Play   76
Sian Hancock, Tutor, Bristol Baptist College

6. Console Champion: Playing with Technology   87
Andy Robertson, freelance video game expert

7. Events Manager: Big Dreams and Nuts and Bolts   98
Carolyn Edwards, Children and Youth Adviser, Diocese of York

8. Hoodie: Spiritual Direction, Silence and Prayer   109
Barbara Meardon, Consultant Adviser for Work with Children and Families

9. Favourite Teacher: Learning the Tenets of Our Faith   121
Howard Worsley, Tutor and Vice Principal in Mission, Trinity College, Bristol

10. Family Picnic: Intergenerational Working   136
Sam Richards, Head of Children's and Youth Work for the United Reformed Church

11. Superhero, Advocate and Idol   147
Ruth Radley, Honorary Chaplain, Birmingham Women's and Children's
Hospital and Mission Partner, Church Mission Society

12. Hard-nosed Head Teacher   161
Michael Wells, retired teacher and Scripture Union Evangelist

13. Falling Leaf Catcher: Experiencing Awe and Wonder with Children   171
David M. Csinos, Assistant Professor of Practical Theology,
Atlantic School of Theology, Halifax, Nova Scotia, Canada

14. Perspectives on Child Theology   180
Keith J. White, Mill Grove, a Christian residential community

THE CONTRIBUTORS   191

INDEX   194

INTRODUCTION
All of God's Children
Sally Nash

As a child, I loved stories where worlds got transformed or made better, and the happy ending that gave me hope. However, not all stories were like that. When I think back to some of the stories I heard and read, it becomes clear that the world was and can, at times, be a challenging place for children (as well as a place of wonder and delight). This has always been so. When we read the Bible, we hear about Moses, the baby being left for someone else to find because Pharaoh had decreed Hebrew male babies were to be drowned at birth (Exodus 2.1–10). The early life of Jesus was disrupted as Mary and Joseph fled to Egypt because of Herod's desire to kill a potential rival (Matthew 2.13–23). We remember the slaughter of the innocent children by Herod as part of the wider Christmas story each year in a world where official statistics suggest that 7000 newborn babies still die every day, mainly from preventable causes (UNICEF 2017).

The Good Childhood Report, published each year by The Children's Society, offers an insight into children's wellbeing in the UK, and recounts how one million children have seven or more serious problems in their lives. The wider context of governmental policy on children and how they are viewed and valued in the world does have an impact, even if sometimes unconsciously, on how we may view children in the Church. There is still some truth in Westerhoff's observation that, 'The discovery of childhood [over the past two centuries] has produced a serious problem; children are not valued for what they *are*, but only for what they can *become*. The less potential a child has, the less value she or he assumes' (1980, p.16). Some of the narrative currently seems to be around wanting children, so we still have a Church in the future when they are adults, rather than valuing what they offer now.

It is often confusing being a child. For example, Collier observes that 'we encourage and recognise creativity and curiosity, empowering children to flourish [yet sometimes] we label the same intrinsic drive as "naughty" etc. and prefer children who are passive, harmless and not disruptive' (2009, p.66). While this may be a generalisation, I am aware of people who have given up on church because they do not appreciate the disapproval communicated if their child is one who wants to do more than be seen but not heard.

A reading of the Old and New Testaments gives a range of examples of how children have significance to God and are part of God's mission, such as:

- Samuel hearing the voice of God (1 Samuel 3)

- David, a child, defeating Goliath (1 Samuel 17)

- two widows having their sons raised from the dead by Elijah and Elisha (1 Kings 17.2; 2 Kings 4)

- Josiah, a child King who was significant in reforming religion and politics (2 Kings 22; 2 Chronicles 34)

- Esther, an orphan child who went on to become a Queen and save her people (Esther 2)

- Jeremiah, called by God as a child (Jeremiah 1)

- Jesus putting a child in the midst and commending others to be like a child (Matthew 18.2–4)

- Jesus talking about the Kingdom of Heaven belonging to children (Matthew 19.14)

- Jesus welcoming and blessing children (Mark 10.13–16)

- Timothy being encouraged not to let people despise him because of his youth (1 Timothy 4.12).

Such examples encourage us to consider children when we are equipping the saints for works of service (Ephesians 4.12) and considering who is engaged within the Great Commission (Matthew 28.16–20) (Kozhuharov 2016, pp.224–226).

Positively, research demonstrates the significance and importance of spirituality in the development of children (Miller 2015c), albeit spirituality has many definitions. Here I would like to start with Swinton's (2001, p.25) five central features of what 'spirituality' is: meaning, values, transcendence, connecting, and becoming. The benefits of engaging with spirituality are beginning to be disseminated through popular media too, thus an article for parents in *Time* magazine states that:

> A strong new body of science, developed during the last decade to what we now consider to be a level of certainty, demonstrates, first, that any sort of spirituality becomes a source of health and thriving for kids and, second, that the lack of spirituality in families and youth culture can be a big source of suffering. (Miller 2015b)

Churches are usually places that are comfortable talking about the spiritual and that offer activities and learning which can positively contribute to the spiritual development of children. This is a vital element of all provision, and helping children develop their spirituality and spiritual strength can bring lifelong benefits.

Underpinning principles for work with children in the Church

While this book has many different authors, there are some underpinning principles that for us are significant in work with children in the Church:

- Based on Genesis 1.26–27, all children are of equal value as unique creations made in the image of God and are worthy of dignity and respect (Bunge 2009); they are 'spiritual beings in a relationship with God...whole persons born in connection with God' (Bonner 2015, p.32).

- All children have assets that are their particular strengths, abilities, skills, talents and capabilities which they bring to our work alongside them (Wilson, Mott and Batman 2004); they also have spiritual assets: trusting; heart knowing and validating; direct transcendent experience; encouraging; and a natural love of nature, of spiritual ritual, prayer, and right action, and of the family as special (Miller 2015a).

- Children are innately spiritual and engaging with their spirituality has a positive impact on other areas of their wellbeing such as emotional, social and cognitive aspects (Hay and Nye 2006; Miller 2015a); holistic approaches engaging with the whole person are beneficial (Kozhuharov 2016).

- We work with children's spirituality regardless of where they are on their journey of Christian faith and discipleship while seeking to support children who are choosing to transition into an owned personal Christian faith that impacts their whole lives.

- Jesus is often found paying particular attention to those on the margins – children's ministry should reflect this and be inclusive of all of God's children. Being excluded is painful and the subsequent wounds can take a long time to heal. Jesus 'had an obvious and often surprising preference for those the rest of the world rejected. He treated them with honor, healed their wounds and called them friends' (Pemberton 2015, p.233).

- Context is significant, and the children's ministry that we engage in has to take account of where our ministry, and those with whom we work, is situated. That is why this is not a 'how to do children's ministry' book but rather, here are some lenses through which to see children's ministry and consider how they may be enacted in your own setting.

- It is not just the responsibility of those who lead and volunteer in children's ministry to engage with children; the whole of the Church can welcome, encourage and give children a sense of value and belonging, and this is important for them (Kozhuharov 2016).

There for the long haul

In an era of cuts in public spending on children, in the UK at least, it may be that the Church is the only institution in some communities offering open-access provision for children and young people. It is also one that can offer a long-term presence, and while employed clergy and workers may come and go, there are usually people within the congregation who offer a continuity of presence and welcome. Children benefit from being part of a wider web of relationships outside of the family, and research on this suggests that developmental relationships are helpful. These are expressed from the child's perspective (Roehlkepartain et al. 2017, p.4)[1] as:

- Express care – be dependable, listen, believe in me, be warm, encourage me.

- Challenge growth – expect my best, stretch me, hold me accountable, reflect on my failures.

---

1   See also www.search-institute.org/downloadable/DevRel_Framework-1-Pager-04-26-2017.pdf

- Provide support – navigate, empower, advocate, set boundaries.

- Share power – expect me, include me, collaborate with me, let me lead.

- Expand possibilities – inspire, broaden horizons, connect.

Looking at a list like this shows how the whole Church can seek to be offering such relationships, opting in at a place where children feel comfortable individually, but also at the structural level having a conversation as to how they are included and integrated, bearing in mind good safeguarding practice.

While we may struggle to see the difference we or our church are making, when you consider all the work with children that happens in the name of the Church, it is a significant contribution to ministry and mission, as Jesus says in Matthew 18.5, 'Whoever welcomes one such child in my name welcomes me.' We cannot overestimate the importance of providing or being a safe place for children. White notes that security 'is the primal need. Without security there is no safe base for exploration, relationships, play and development... In biblical terms we note that a "safe place" (from Eden to the Ark, the Promised Land and the New Jerusalem) is the most fundamental image of salvation. "I go to prepare a place for you"' (2011, p.91). White (2011) then identifies significance, boundaries, community and creativity as other needs that together can be used to assess the effectiveness of any approach to caring for children. These are some of the issues we need to bear in mind as we shape our children's ministry and what they may look like in practice. White's principles are based on his many years of working with children at Mill Grove,[2] which functions as an extended family and residential community. This long-term engagement was very much focused on the holistic needs of the child rather than solely their spiritual or faith development. Holistic child development has as its aim transformation and at its fullest this may involve transforming communities and even aspects of society too (Kozhuharov 2016, pp.258–261). Transformation of an individual happens in community and includes 'physical, social, moral, aesthetic, creative and spiritual aspects of personal growth' and participation by individuals in the community (Kozhuharov 2016, p.259).

---

2   See www.millgrove.org.uk

Using metaphor to inform and understand children's ministry

The main part of this book uses a series of metaphors to give a glimpse into different aspects of ministry and mission with children. We have chosen these different metaphors because of their significance in thought (Lakoff and Johnson 1980) and in Scripture. When we read John's Gospel we have a series of ways of understanding Jesus: the good shepherd, the vine, bread of life, living water, and so on. The metaphors that we use will impact the way that we do ministry with children, and it is likely that we have metaphors that impact what we do even if we do not articulate them. Take this example: 'Would I teach "pilgrims" the same way I would teach "sponges"? What difference does it make if I envision my learners as passive, inanimate sponges or as active, growing, relational living beings? What are sponge-like activities? What are pilgrim activities? Does any of this matter?' (May *et al.* 2005, p.6). We believe it *does* matter, and encourage you as you go through the book to reflect on what your metaphors might be for the different dimensions of ministry discussed.

A further example is how we see our role as leaders with children and young people. Passive metaphors include expert, authority, boss, evaluator and funnel holder (to facilitate pouring things in), whereas active ones include shepherd, farmer or gardener, fellow pilgrim, guide or friend. These latter metaphors support a more active and engaged approach that values learning by experience and sees learners as significant in the process. The passive metaphors are similar to Freire's (1996) banking approach that sees children as containers that need filling up. Similarly, Bonner suggests that 'as those created in the image of God, children are not merely blank slates, spongers, or empty vessels that come to us ready to be filled as passive recipients of spiritual information. Children are born to us as active makers of spiritual meaning. They make meaning in unique and personalized ways' (2015, p.33). Denying this depersonalises children and sets them up as something less than God created them to be, and their agency is denied (Bonner 2015).

May and her colleagues (2005, pp.10–22) go on to identify some overarching metaphors of ministry with children in Table 0.1. This may be a helpful starting place for beginning to review where your existing provision is.

TABLE 0.1: METAPHOR-BASED MODELS OF CHILDREN'S MINISTRY

Model	Strengths	Weaknesses
School model	Familiar, easy to organise, knowing content emphasised, straightforward to deliver, some children can build good relationships with their teacher	Focus on cognitive over affective domain and character development, too close to school for some, little active learning, can be hard to recruit teachers as people do not feel qualified, rarely takes account of individuals
Gold star/win a prize model	Popular with competitive children, can produce good short-term results, volunteers who enjoy competition attracted to it, values enthusiasm	Stressful for non-competitive children, based on extrinsic rather than intrinsic motivation, can devalue cooperation, learning often disliked by those who struggle at school, overstimulating for some or creates animosity, prize can be more important than content
Carnival model (have fun, high spot of the week)	Teaching is entertaining and engaging, children enjoy coming and may invite friends, fun is valued, object lessons and analogies easy to integrate	Can be disconnect between environment and purpose – entertainment focus similar to culture at large, lack of opportunity for awe and wonder, overwhelming for some, can be expensive, needs high commitment and skill from leaders
Pilgrims' journey model (people of different ages influence each other on a journey that lasts a lifetime)	Learning opportunities are part of life and formative, learning is intentional and aimed at spiritual growth, teachers and learners are fellow pilgrims with teachers functioning as guides and companions, all ages participate holistically, flexible	Can be challenging for those leading, learning may be hard to assess, not likely to attract large numbers, can be less systematic
Dance with God model (relational model – child's living relationship with God in the world)	Draws on concept that faith is a process and we grow in it, high view of child and God's view of child, assumes children can encounter God with awe and wonder, learning built around authentic tasks, lifelong process	Can be difficult for some leaders to know how to facilitate, does not always provide opportunities for children to make a clear commitment to follow Jesus

As well as considering models of ministry it can be helpful to reflect on how we frame our own role. Bonner offers the metaphor of the spiritual pedagogue (2015, pp.41–42). This model is one that can stand alongside many of the metaphors in this book. He notes that unlike contemporary usage meaning teacher, pedagogue in ancient Mediterranean cultures described someone who was 'child tender…a custodian for the young' (Bonner 2015, p.42), who may journey alongside a child for a decade or more as their constant companion and who served as a moral guide. While this may not be practical in its entirety in contemporary contexts, it is possible to consider a spiritual pedagogue inviting 'the child into active participation in the kingdom where together we serve others and live out God's love' with the consequence that as the child matures, they begin to see that 'their faith is beautiful and alive in God, they have value and are valued, their presence matters, they are active contributors to life of the community, they are beloved of God' (Bonner 2015, p.42). And importantly, this model acknowledges the reciprocity in the relationship understanding that they are both transformed and influenced in that relationship as they inspire that in the child (Bonner 2015). In the remainder of the book practitioners offer their understanding of different roles and dimensions of children's ministry and how this journey can be enhanced.

An overview of the rest of the book

We hope that this book will be of interest to those who work directly with children, those who have oversight of such work and everyone who has a passion to see effective work with children happening in our churches and through Christian organisations – this may include parents, grandparents and other family members. This book is relevant for churches of all denominations and traditions interested in engaging in or developing their work with children, both inside and outside of the Church. We hope we are broadening horizons and offering fresh insights into how the whole Church may work with all of God's children.

QUESTIONS FOR REFLECTION AND DISCUSSION

- How do you engage children's spirituality through your current provision?

- What sort of place are we preparing through our children's ministry for them to be able to come and flourish?

- What metaphors are you aware of in your own and your church's understanding of children's ministry?

- Which metaphor model would you like to explore further? How might you introduce elements of that into your current approach?

References and further reading

Bonner, S. (2015) 'Understanding Childhood Spirituality.' In R. Bruner and D.K. Pemberton (eds) *Along the Way: Conversations about Children and Faith* (pp.31–43). Abilene, TX: Abilene Christian University Press.

Bunge, M.J. (2009) 'Historical Perspectives on Children in the Church.' In J. Collier (ed.) *Toddling to the Kingdom* (pp.98–113). London: Child Theology Movement.

Children's Society, The (2017) *The Good Childhood Report 2017*. Available at www.childrenssociety. org.uk/the-good-childhood-report-2017

Collier, J. (ed.) (2009) *Toddling to the Kingdom*. London: Child Theology Movement.

Freire, P. (1996) *Pedagogy of the Oppressed*. London: Penguin.

Griffiths, M. (2017) *Changing Lives: The Essential Guide to Ministry with Children and Families*. Oxford: Monarch.

Hay, D. and Nye, R. (2006) *The Spirit of the Child*. London: Jessica Kingsley Publishers.

Kozhuharov, V. (2016) *Child, Church, Mission*. London: WTL Publications.

Lakoff, G. and Johnson, M. (1980) *Metaphors We Live By*. Chicago, IL: University of Chicago Press.

May, S., Posterski. B., Stonehouse, C. and Cannell, L. (2005) *Children Matter*. Grand Rapids, MI: Eerdmans.

Miller, L. (2015a) *The Spiritual Child*. New York: St Martin's Press.

Miller, L. (2015b) 'Why kids who believe in something are happier and healthier.' *Time*, 17 April. Available at http://time.com/3825083/why-kids-who-believe-in-something-are-happier-and-healthier

Miller, L. (ed.) (2015c) 'Guest Editor note.' *Journal of Religion and Health 54*(3).

Pemberton, D.K. (2015) 'Holy Hospitality: Following the Call of Jesus to Welcome ALL Children.' In R. Bruner and D.K. Pemberton (eds) *Along the Way: Conversations about Children and Faith* (pp.219–233). Abilene, TX: Abilene Christian University Press.

Roehlkepartain, E.C., Pekel, K., Syvertsen, A.K., Sethi, J., Sullivan, T.K. and Scales, P.C. (2017) *Relationships First: Creating Connections that Help Young People Thrive*. Minneapolis, MN: Search Institute.

Swinton, J. (2001) *Spirituality and Mental Health Care: Rediscovering a 'Forgotten' Dimension*. London: Jessica Kingsley Publishers.

UNICEF (2017) *Levels and Trends in Child Mortality Report*. Available at www.unicef.org/publications/index_101071.html

Westerhoff, J. (1980) *Bringing Up Children in the Christian Faith*. San Francisco, CA: HarperSanFrancisco.

White, K.J. (2011) *The Growth of Love*. Abingdon: Barnabas.

White, K.J. and Willmer, H. (2009) 'A Theoretical Typology of Children's Needs.' In J. Collier (ed.) *Toddling to the Kingdom* (pp.90–97). London: Child Theology Movement.

Wilson, L.L., Mott, D.W. and Batman, D. (2004) 'The asset-based context matrix: A tool for assessing children's learning opportunities and participation in natural environments.' *Topics in Early Childhood Special Education 24*(2), 110–120.

Chapter 1

TRAIN DRIVER

Growing through Experience

Isobel MacDougall

Introduction

> Oscar is seven years old. Never be fooled by his small size – he is
> strong and very fit. He is a Man City supporter, wears an Agüero
> football shirt and is always on the move. When he was six weeks
> old, Oscar was very ill with bronchiolitis and was in hospital for
> two weeks. As a result, he has asthma and has had recurrent chest
> infections – but this has never stopped him from doing sport. Oscar
> has an older sister Hermione and a younger brother Harry and a new
> baby sister Seren. Oscar enjoys sharing his passion for sport with
> his dad, and his interest in art and books with his mum. They are
> important people in his life. We will be discovering more about Oscar
> throughout this chapter.

What do you think of when you hear the words 'train driver'? This will
depend on your age, interests and possibly your childhood experiences. It
could be steam trains, like Thomas the Tank Engine, or the Settle to Carlisle
Express. Perhaps it's Eurostar, and memories of exciting holidays or visits to
Paris. Maybe you are thinking about the Orient Express, a romantic journey,
or one surrounded by mystery, intrigue and exploration of the East. Perhaps
it is a more political view, with train drivers becoming redundant, making
way for driver-less trains. This metaphor of the 'train driver' elicits different
perspectives – changing landscapes and arousing different emotions. A train
driver takes passengers on a journey from a known start to a determined
destination, but the routes may be very different and unexpected. In this
chapter we are going on such a journey as we explore the concept of
childhood. We will consider different views of childhood, issues of agency
and power relations, and the process of being a child as an infant through

to adolescence. Each child is different, and their journey through life will be unique, even the lives of identical twins.

As this is a complex subject, and the object of much research over the years, in this chapter we will only be raising the key issues, many of which will be explored in greater depth in the following chapters. We begin with the question: what is a child? The chapter then considers the holistic nature of childhood including neuroscience, developmental psychology and the social construction of childhood. Throughout the chapter different theoretical perspectives are discussed and a range of theorists introduced. Oscar and his siblings are used as a case study to illustrate the development and learning processes in the first seven years of life. A famous Jesuit saying states, 'Give me a child until he is seven, and I will show you the man.' As we will see, the first years of life are a critical foundation and can affect later life.

It is important that you engage with the ideas and concepts that are discussed and reflect on your own views, assumptions and beliefs about children and adolescence. As we work with children and young people, we are often reminded about issues in our own childhoods. The relationships, experiences and events of our lives have helped to shape who we are and what we believe. Remaining reflective and willing to consider other views and paradigms is important. Look out for articles about children and adolescents in the news and think about the way that the media, government and the Church talk about them. What is the view of current society? Before you continue reading this chapter, note down the dominant views of childhood you have learned or read about, or seen portrayed through social media, television, films and books.

What is a child?

What does childhood mean to you? What do you think influences childhood? It may be helpful to reflect on your own childhood experiences in answering these questions.

If we looked at legislation or the literature to answer the questions, we may have very different answers about the ages when childhood starts and ends. Look up the ages at which it is legal to vote, join the Armed Forces, get married, have a sexual relationship, get a mortgage and buy alcohol in a pub. There is no fixed age for all these events that may be considered to be adult activities. Does a child become an adolescent when they become a teenager at 13 or when they move from primary to secondary school?

Esther Rantzen recently carried out a survey to see why fewer children were contacting Childline even though other research has highlighted the growing numbers of children suffering from stress. She discovered that children as young as ten no longer considered themselves to be a 'child'. As a result, she is developing a new app for phones and internet access called 'Is it ok?', so that children and young people of all ages will feel confident to seek help.

Frone, cited in Waller (2009, p.2), suggests that 'Childhood may be defined as the life period during which a human being is regarded as a child and the cultural, social and economic characteristics of that period.' Childhood can be viewed as a social construction, therefore changing through time and place, but it is investigated by exploring development and learning. There are many different theoretical perspectives on human development, including behaviourist, development psychologist, constructionist and social constructionist theories. Although development is holistic, with all aspects of development having an impact on the other, we will start by exploring the development of the brain, as this is critical to the developing child and future development. We will then briefly discuss other theoretical perspectives of development.

Neuroscience

In recent years neuroscience has enabled researchers to discover a more accurate understanding of the developing brain. Our brains are comprised of a hundred billion neurons and glia cells. Neurons have fibrous branches called dendrites that transit information to other neurons and axons, which receive incoming signals. Repeated signals are continuously processed by the neurons and stronger pathways develop, creating a complex network in the brain. The axons become covered in the myelin sheath, made up of high percentages of fat. This sheath helps the information to be passed on from one neuron to another, travelling along the axon, across a synapse and onto the next neuron (Gopnik, Meltzoff and Kuhl 1999). Repetition enables the pathways to become stronger. Pathways that are no longer used die off as the brain prunes its rapidly developing network.[1] Neuroscience has identified that the brain develops through social interaction, and that by the age of three the brain is 80 per cent developed.

Gerhardt (2004) discusses the importance of the early social experience on brain development in the young child. She states that very early social experiences affect the amygdala, one of the core structures of the emotional brain. Social experiences in very young children can

---

1   Watch the video 'How the human brain works' produced by the University of Bristol at www.youtube.com/watch?v=9UukcdU258A

strengthen or undermine connections and neural pathways in the higher prefrontal brain areas, which have a key role in managing the core emotion structures. This regulation depends on the relationship between the infant and their main caregivers – for example, when a distressed baby is comforted, or a restless baby is stimulated, biochemicals such as oxytocin and serotonin are released, enabling the baby to feel safe and relaxed. While stress causes a rise in the levels of cortisol in the body and is necessary to help cope with immediate distress or stressful situations., the child who is not comforted, or whose needs are not met, will produce chronically high levels of this hormone, which can go on to have a negative effect on the nervous system throughout life.

Zeedyk (2010) states that babies develop as a consequence of relationships as well as their genetic codes. Unlike the animal kingdom, babies' brains are flexible and can adapt to different environments. Previously, it was thought that the brain was fixed by the age of three, and although it is now recognised that the brain continues to develop throughout childhood, with another period of rapid development in puberty, Zeedyk (2010) suggests that recent research has shown that particular pathways are laid down in relation to a particular environment and become established in adulthood. The home environment shapes the neural pathways in the brain – for example, where there is domestic violence, the baby or young child constantly needs to be alert to possible threats and determine where this threat will come from. Zeedyk comments that if a child from this type of environment goes into nursery or school, they will still be alert to possible threats and find it difficult to sit, concentrate and focus on learning. This reinforces the importance of people working with children knowing about children's home environments and being able to tune into the child.

Robinson (2010) discusses the importance of attunement, in which the primary carers recognise and identify the needs of individual children and are able to respond to them. Roberts (2010) develops this idea further, stating that young children thrive best with companionable relationships, bound together with love and affection. This consistent, responsive care of young children supports the development of the prefrontal cortex, which enables young children to control their impulses, pay attention and to develop emotional and social skills (Gerhardt 2004). Thus these early relationships are foundational for healthy emotional and social development, supporting building relationships throughout life and providing a good base for learning and holistic development.

So the development of the brain with its links to emotional and social development is critical within the development of the whole person.

Significantly, if we consider the story of creation, God made an amazing world, but the pinnacle of his creation was the creation of humankind. Within Christianity, the story of creation is written down in the first book of the Bible, and Genesis 2 states that God wanted the man and woman he created to have a relationship with him. So we were made for relationships. The evidence for this is in the design of the brain and the way that it develops through social interaction, particularly love and affection. Relationships are therefore essential for human growth and development.

> Oscar enjoys spending time with his baby sister Seren, who is just four weeks old. He gets close to her and talks to her softly. She holds his gaze, mimicking the movements of his mouth and makes baby noises. When she is crying, Oscar talks to her, and she is soothed – unless she is hungry!

Theories of development

Behaviourism was a popular theoretical approach to development rooted in psychology, based on theorists such as Skinner, Watson and Pavlov. Strategies for managing children's behaviour, such as reward charts and time out, are based on these theories. In the 1960s, Piaget's research on children's cognitive development introduced a constructivist approach, in which children are seen as actively involved in learning. Piaget proposed that children assimilate and accommodate new experiences in order to learn. The work of Piaget influenced education in the UK, encouraging teachers to recognise the importance of being an active learner, but also identifying the different developmental stages that children pass through.

> Oscar, Hermione and Harry watched the 'old' Star Wars films for a movie night. They had been given some of the Star Wars characters. Over the following days, the children re-enacted and extended the storyline, using other props to substitute for the Millennium Falcon and X-wing fighters.

Vygotsky, a Russian philosopher and psychologist, proposed that children are not just active learners; they are also social learners. As a sociocultural theorist, Vygotsky (1986) was far more interested in the child as a social actor, learning alongside more knowledgeable others in a collective context. He considered the socio-historical context as essential in the social learning process, the child drawing on their historical context as well as the current environmental one. Vygotsky proposed that children are cultural participants within communities, living at a particular time in history and place. He hypothesised that inner speech, essential for supporting higher mental processes, develops separately from the child's external speech, but is dependent on external factors. Thought development is dependent on language. Verbal thought, he proposed, was not innate, but learned through cultural historical processes. Children solve practical tasks with the help of their speech as well as their eyes and hands. Vygotsky noted through observations of children that when they were confronted with problems that were slightly too complicated for them, they used a range of strategies to help them, such as tools, speech to others, speech to themselves or speech to the object to master the problem. Oscar and his siblings drew on their new knowledge about the Star Wars story and used language, props and each other to extend their learning and explore their imaginations.

Changing landscapes of childhood

But what are the dominant views of children in the West? In your notes, how did you suggest that they are perceived by society today? The dominant discourse of childhood in the UK has been based on child development theories arising from the discipline of psychology, and is one in which the child is seen as relatively powerless and in need of adult protection. This discourse holds certain images of the child – the child becoming the adult, passive and biologically programmed to grow and develop from child to adult with the help of knowledgeable adults; the innocent child, needing to be protected from the corrupt world by rescuing adults; and the redemptive child, seen as the saviour of their world by being redeemed through high-quality children's services and the care of their family.

These dominant themes of rationality, naturalness and universality, based on developmental psychology and biologically determined, have resulted in an evolutionary model from simplicity in childhood to complexity in adulthood, in which passive children go through the process of socialisation to reach adulthood.

In 1994, Postman wrote that childhood in the twentieth century was 'disappearing'. This view could be construed as being supported by government concerns of family breakdown, the commercialisation and sexualisation of childhoods and the need to get 'back to basics'. Jenks (2005) suggested that the 'age of innocence' is over and the concept of childhood is open to negotiation by different interested parties. In fact, a landmark case shattered the view of the innocent, weak child. The murder of James Bulger in 1999 by two ten-year-old boys shocked the nation and ignited the debate around childhood as being socially constructed, suggesting that the socio-economic background, family, the media and culture shape children's lives. This discussion, that childhood is contestable and culturally variable, continues through high-profile cases such as the attack on two boys in Doncaster by two other boys (Walker and Wainright 2010), where the childhoods of the children were debated in an attempt to understand what happened. Living in the postmodern global world of the twenty-first century therefore requires new ways of thinking and understanding knowledge, engaging with cultural diversity and cross-cultural dialogue.

The view of the child as a co-constructor of knowledge, identity and culture emerged as social constructionist and postmodern perspectives were explored within sociology, philosophy and psychology, when developmental psychology was being critiqued and the comparative movement in psychology was gaining popularity (Montgomery 2003). The postmodern world is described as being socially constructed and social construction is always context-specific and value-laden, and its proponents challenge the values of modernity, and the context in which developmental psychology is situated. Postmodernity claims that there is no absolute truth, no absolute reality waiting to be discovered. In fact, postmodernism problematises dualistic thinking, considering both/and rather than either/or, and is characterised by a critique of previously held universal truths often referred to as grand narratives.

Within this framework, Dahlberg, Moss and Pence (2007) discuss the need to problematise the dominance of 'Western' discourses and their influence on practice today, and to see them in perspective, consider their limitations, acknowledge their assumptions and question their reasoning. They agree with other academics that there is an increasing realisation that childhood is constructed by society and that this is dependent on diverse socio-economic, political, cultural and historical contexts. With a greater focus on children's rights, legislation and education has highlighted the importance of listening to children and young people and considering their views about issues relating to their lives.

Oscar has recently been 'spotted' by a London football club and trains with them every week. He watches 'Match of the Day' with his dad on catch-up TV. Oscar is 'gutted' that he didn't get a Nintendo DS for Christmas and doesn't have an iPad like 'the rest of his friends'. There are over 30 different languages spoken in his school, and some of the children are refugees.

Children and young people's lives have changed dramatically in the last century. In the twenty-first-century UK factors such as children and work, the child as a consumer and as a citizen with rights, child refugees, increasing access to social media, changing attitudes towards sexuality, access to education and outdoor spaces and the need for children and young people to achieve well in order to provide a secure future economy are just some of the aspects about childhood and adolescence that need to be explored by people who are working with children and young people. Globalisation has also changed the world, and we need to take account of a global perspective (Montgomery 2013).

There are many interesting accounts by anthropologists studying children and their families across the world, demonstrating diverse cultural attitudes and discourses of childhood. You may have grown up in a family culture that is not White British or be working within multicultural contexts. It is critical that we find out about different attitudes to the period of life known as childhood, and it is important that we do not become Eurocentric in our beliefs about development, but consider multicultural views. Listening to the young people and children we are working with, hearing their views and getting to know their families, will be a valuable source of information.

Who is driving the train?

Teachers, youth workers and adults who work with children play an important role in the lives of children and young people. Think back to significant adults in your life and consider what it was that was valuable for you. Parents and carers are also highly significant, and the vast majority are 'good enough' parents, providing care and security for their children (Chapter 5 explores the importance of parents and families in more depth). However, working with children and young people requires us to work within the boundaries of government legislation, children's rights (UN 1989) and policy directives for the organisations we work for. Being 'professional' is critical, and making sure that we work within professional parameters will ensure safety for all. Professionalism is a complex and ambiguous concept, and may well change with each organisation, but issues such as ethical practice, respect, inclusive practice and safeguarding are non-negotiable. It is important that all adults working with children and young people not only read the policies of their organisation but also implement and monitor them. It is everyone's responsibility to safeguard children and young people.

So does this mean that the adult is in control and has power over those in their care? A careful reading of children's rights makes it clear that children and young people must be treated fairly and be participants in issues that affect them. The term 'supervision' is often used when looking after children. In a dictionary this is defined as 'oversee activity or oversee people'. If we think back to neuroscience and the importance of relationships on the developing brain, relationships are at the heart of all we do, but need to be reciprocal.

As we have seen earlier in this chapter, Vygotsky proposed that we learn within our sociocultural contexts – learning and development being a social process as children and young people learn alongside more knowledgeable others. These may be adults or peers. Children and young people also learn with their peers as they co-construct knowledge, exploring and discovering together, and they may learn alone. Language is an important tool for developing thinking as well as communicating with others, but it is not just family, teachers and friends that influence and help to shape the developing identities of the child or young person; the wider environments within society shape us all.

> Oscar has a large extended family and enjoys playing with his cousins, going out with his various aunts and uncles, staying with his grandparents and visiting his great granny. He has a wide circle of friends through school, church and family friends. He attends the asthma clinic at the hospital and has regular visits to the dentist. As Oscar is in Year 2, he will be doing SATs at school this year, as part of government policy for education. Oscar's family sponsors a child in Uganda through a charity and his family has friends living in other countries.

So what about you? Think about the influences on your own early life, then read about Bronfenbrenner's Ecological Systems Theory (1979) and study Figure 1.1. Bronfenbrenner demonstrated how all the layers of society around people influence them, even global influences. And the influence is two-way, from the outside in and the inside out. For example, climate change is affecting the physical environment and challenging the energy, transport, industries and lifestyles we lead. Try to plot those influences into his concentric circles – the microsystem, which includes those closest to you; the mesosystem, which includes your immediate community – and continue to consider the geographical, political and historical context of your early years. Consider how these different influences have shaped who you have become.

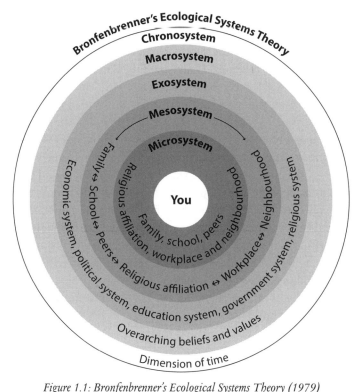

Figure 1.1: Bronfenbrenner's Ecological Systems Theory (1979)

It is important that people who work with children and young people are aware of the spheres of influence. It is also important that, where possible, we work with families, so that we get to know what is important to them and how to provide consistent care and support. As for the question, 'Who is driving the train?', who do you think it should be?

Foucault (1980), a French philosopher, analysed various types of power including sovereign power and disciplinary power. Sovereign power is the binary model, where there is a ruler and the ruled, where what is legal and illegal are clearly distinguishable. Subjects, such as managers, teachers and workers with children and young people, are the visible agents of sovereign power. In contrast, disciplinary power is less visible, shaping subjects with or without their consent. This power is not combative as in sovereign power, but is subtler. Disciplinary power is used to train and encourage conformity through normalisation to the accepted norms in a given society or context. This may be through expectations of manners, behaviour or following particular traditions or routines. Disciplinary power guides subjects towards a desired outcome set by the authority power.

Foucault outlined specific properties of power. Power relations are both intentional and non-subjective, and power is exercised in the interaction between force and resistance. Foucault stated that it is this resistance that produces power relations. Understanding Foucault's theories about power relations will enable adults working with children and young people to reflect on the power relations that exist within their sphere of work and the type of relationship they establish within the organisation and the young person or child. While the adult has responsibility for safeguarding, relationships must be respectful and reciprocal. Perhaps the driver of the train changes depending on the context and situation. Oscar's parents provide clear boundaries for their children, but they listen to them and reason with them rather than taking an autocratic stance. There are different styles of parenting just as there are different styles of working with children and young people. Read about these and consider which one adheres to children's rights, respects children's views and safeguards children effectively. Children and young people are growing up in a world that is rapidly changing and is very different from the world you yourself grew up in.

Into a brave new world

As stated in the United Nations' Convention on the Rights of the Child (UN 1989, Article 3):

> In all actions concerning children, whether undertaken by public or private social welfare institutions, courts of law, administrative authorities or legislative bodies, the best interests of the child shall be a primary consideration.

When the concept of children's rights was conceived after the First World War, it was hoped that the needs of children would be protected and that children would be able to grow up in a just society (Montgomery 2003).

However, research carried out in the twenty-first century suggests that children are growing up in an ever-unequal society, and organisations working with young people report rising levels of mental health issues. Read, in particular, the reports listed in the References at the end of this chapter from The Children's Society (2017), UN (1989) and the Joseph Rowntree Foundation (2016a, b). These will inform you about issues related to poverty, education and health. Make notes of the key facts and consider how they impact on social and emotional wellbeing, opportunities for achievement, and the life chances of children and young people.

So many changes have taken place in the world in the last century. Scientific research has produced treatments for serious illnesses, immunisation has prevented other illnesses, technology has enabled men to go to the moon, developed the internet and invented mobile phones, and social media is now the popular form of communication throughout the world. This has been beneficial in many ways, but there are also challenges and concerns. Read the recommended articles on social media and consider the ramifications of, for example, sexting for children and young people. They are living in a world where something private can go viral in minutes, exposing their privacy to the world (you can read more about this in Chapters 4 and 7). Another issue that shapes who we are becoming and how we position ourselves in society is gender. Read *The Good Childhood Report* (The Children's Society 2017) and the Department for Education report (Lessof *et al.* 2016), and identify the issues related to gender that are currently affecting children and adolescents.

So how do we help children and young people to protect themselves and survive in this rapidly changing world? Developing positive self-esteem and a positive sense of self is critical. These will help the growing child and developing young person to face the challenges of an uncertain and ever-changing world. Adults working with them can support them by encouraging resilience, emotional intelligence, spiritual growth and development and self-awareness. A strong sense of who we are with our different identities provides us with the resources to embrace challenge.

Erikson, a psychologist, built on the work of Freud and proposed a psychoanalytic theory of psychosocial development. He suggested that there are eight stages from infancy to adulthood. He stated that during each stage, the child or young person experiences 'a psychosocial crisis' that could create either a positive or negative outcome for personality development. Erikson stressed the role of culture and society, and stated that any conflicts within these crises take place in the 'ego'. The ego develops through the process of resolving social crises, producing a sense of trust in others and developing a sense of self. Like Piaget and other psychologists such as Freud, Erikson maintained that the development of personality matures in a predetermined order, through the eight stages, each stage building on the previous one. Erikson was interested in how the socialisation of children affects their developing sense of self. Oscar and Hermione are in stage 4, industry or competence versus inferiority. While it is important not to categorise children and young people, both Oscar and Hermione are increasingly competent and skilful, but despite this, they can quickly feel inferior and are very aware of the achievements of others. Competition can be good, but unchecked it can also heighten inferiority at a time when children need to grow in confidence. Harry is in stage 3 and is socialising with others in school and learning how to lead and take the initiative. Erikson suggests that in this stage of initiative versus guilt, children may ask many questions, and if these questions are seen by adults to be trivial or embarrassing, the child may feel guilty for being a nuisance. Seren, just a few weeks old, is in stage 1. She is finding out about her new relationships and making sense of the world around her. She is finding out about trust versus mistrust. Adults who work with children need to be emotionally intelligent and sensitive to the changing needs of children in diverse contexts.

According to Erikson's stages, it is during the teenage years that the identity crisis begins, and only adolescents who are successful in resolving the crisis will be ready to face future challenges in life. Erikson calls this stage identity versus role confusion, stage 5. However, the identity crisis may well be recurring, as we constantly need to redefine ourselves within the ever-changing world. As previously stated, with rapid development in technology, the global economy and changing local and world politics, identity crises are inevitable, and it is anticipated may occur more often than the times when Erikson was researching his theories in the 1960s.

Recognition of the importance of the participation clauses within children's rights, where children and young people have the right to be involved and express their opinions in issues that affect their lives, will help adults working with children and young people to encourage their sense of agency. Making decisions, negotiating conflicts, being independent and taking risks help children and young people to become resilient and ready for a brave new world.

Summary

This chapter has introduced several concepts, ideas and theoretical perspectives. One of the important threads is the notion of the child or young person within their sociocultural, historical and environmental context, with particular reference to Vygotsky and Erikson. Taking a sociocultural stance requires that we consider the different discourses of childhood, the spheres of influence around the child and the changing world of the twenty-first century. All these topics are both important and vast, and it is therefore critical that you read and research them more widely using the References list in this chapter and other sources within the book.

QUESTIONS FOR REFLECTION AND DISCUSSION

- How can researching a range of theoretical perspectives on development help the child and youth worker to understand the child or young person and the role of the youth worker?

- How does an understanding of the diverse discourses of childhood and cultural diversity help the child and youth worker to understand the child or young person?

- Think about power relations within organisations that you are involved in. How do they affect the way that people work in the organisation? How do they affect the children and young people who attend the organisation?

- What are the main changes that have taken place in the last 60 years in the UK that have had the greatest influence on our society today?

References and further reading

Bronfenbrenner, U. (1979) *The Ecology of Human Development: Experiments by Nature and Design.* Cambridge, MA: Harvard University Press.

Children's Society, The (2017) *The Good Childhood Report.* Available at www.childrenssociety.org.uk/what-we-do/research/the-good-childhood-report

Dahlberg, G., Moss, P. and Pence, A. (2007) *Beyond Quality in Early Childhood Education and Care: Languages of Evaluation.* London: Routledge.

Foucault, M. (1980) *Power/Knowledge: Selected Interviews and Other Writings. 1972–1977.* New York: Vintage.

Gerhardt, S. (2004) *Why Love Matters: How Affection Shapes a Baby's Brain.* London: Routledge.

Gopnik, A., Meltzoff, A. and Kuhl, P. (1999) *How Babies Think.* London: Phoenix.

Gray, C. and MacBlain, S. (2012) *Learning Theories in Childhood.* London: Sage.

Herrera, B. (2016) 'Social media and young people's mental health.' Mental Health Foundation blog, 9 May. Available at www.mentalhealth.org.uk/blog/social-media-and-young-peoples-mental-health

Jenks, C. (2005) *Childhood* (2nd edn). London: Routledge.

Joseph Rowntree Foundation (2016a) *UK Poverty: Causes, Costs and Solutions.* Available at www.jrf.org.uk/report/uk-poverty-causes-costs-and-solutions

Joseph Rowntree Foundation (2016b) *Monitoring Poverty and Social Exclusion 2016.* Available at www.jrf.org.uk/report/monitoring-poverty-and-social-exclusion-2016

Kennedy, M. (2016) 'More than a third of teenage girls in England suffer depression and anxiety.' *The Guardian*, 22 August. Available at www.theguardian.com/society/2016/aug/22/third-teenage-girls-depression-anxiety-survey-trend-truant

Lessof, C., Ross, A., Brind, R., Bell, E. and Newton, S. (2016) *Longitudinal Study of Young People in England Cohort 2: Health and Well-being Wave 2.* Research Report. London: Department for Education. Available at www.gov.uk/government/uploads/system/uploads/attachment_data/file/540563/LSYPE2_w2_research_report.pdf

Montgomery, H. (2003) 'Children in Time and Place.' In M. Woodhead and H. Montgomery (eds) *Understanding Childhood: An Interdisciplinary Approach* (pp.1–52). Milton Keynes: Open University.

Montgomery, H. (2013) 'Interventions and Ideologies.' In H. Montgomery (ed.) *Local Childhoods, Global Issues* (2nd edn) (pp.213–262). Bristol: Policy Press.

Postman, N. (1994) *The Disappearance of Childhood.* New York: Vintage Books.

Roberts, R. (2010) *Well-being from Birth.* London: Sage.

Robinson, M. (2010) *Attunement.* Available at www.youtube.com/watch?v=AAxWDA4XPkE

Udorie, J.E. (2016) 'Social media is harming the mental health of teenagers: The state has to act.' *The Guardian*, 16 September. Available at www.theguardian.com/commentisfree/2015/sep/16/social-media-mental-health-teenagers-government-pshe-lessons

UN (United Nations) (1989) *Convention on the Rights of the Child.* Available at https://downloads.unicef.org.uk/wp-content/uploads/2010/05/UNCRC_united_nations_convention_on_the_rights_of_the_child.pdf?_ga=2.216358549.247692187.1537455708-670060270.1537455708

UNICEF (2016) *Fairness for Children. A League Table of Inequality in Child Well-being in Rich Countries.* Innocenti Report Card 13. Florence: Office of Research-Innocenti. Available at www.unicef-irc.org/publications/pdf/RC13_eng.pdf

Vygotsky, V.W. (1986) *Thought and Language.* Revised and edited by A. Kozulin. Cambridge, MA: MIT Press.

Walker, P. and Wainright, M. (2010) 'Edlington brothers jailed for torture of two boys.' *The Guardian*, 22 January. Available at www.theguardian.com/uk/2010/jan/22/edlington-brothers-jailed-torture-boys

Waller, T. (2009) *An Introduction to Early Childhood: A Multi-disciplinary Approach.* London: Sage.

Zeedyk, S. (2010) *Brain Development.* Available at www.youtube.com/watch?v=2lyjNIIJ0LM

Chapter 2

TEDDY BEAR

Holding the Whispers Shared in the Dark

Paul Nash

Introduction

One of the responsibilities and privileges of working with children is that that we get to support them during some of the most difficult times of their lives. These might be times of loss, bereavement, transition, trauma, abuse or bullying, for example. What I do in this chapter is consider contexts, some key theories and then name and explore some principles of how we can support children going through such experiences.

Contexts

What we might be talking about

- serious illness, death of a family member, friend or significant adult such as a teacher

- family: breakdown, new, mental health, young carers, prison

- illness, disability, accidents

- bullying at school or online

- abuse

- moving school, home

- childhood development

- refugees, war-torn areas

- traumatic events observed on TV or through social media.

Some of these issues would be perceived as normal – transition and change; some as sad – illness and loss; some as unacceptable – bullying and abuse. Gustafsson uses the term 'triangle of chaos' to describe some of these issues, and sees that they largely fall into three categories (cited in Borgman 2003, p.150):

- trauma and confusion within themselves

- disruption and pain of torn families

- chaos within community and family.

What might be going on

When a child does want to share with us some of the difficult dimensions of their life there are a variety of reasons why this may be so. These include: the normal stressors of life and wanting to share them with someone outside of the family; powerlessness in a situation that is hurting them in some way where they are looking for a safe person to talk to; a lack of attachment in some key relationships where they may otherwise be sharing; or the need to make meaning and needing someone to help them with that. They may also have feelings and expressions of anger, sadness, withdrawal, guilt, sleep disorders, questioning self-worth, blame, shame, humiliation, embarrassment, shock and so on that they are struggling to handle.

Developmental levels

Even drilling down and writing a book about children, due to their complex developmental lives we may not be as sharp and concise as would be helpful. Any time there is a child or young person we are engaging with, there is a wide range of issues that we need to take into account. Many of the issues discussed in this chapter are hidden, and we will sometimes not see them unless we ask; sadly it is helpful if we just expect to find them.

Loss and grief

Loss is a significant issue in the lives of children, and there are six main ways in which loss might be experienced (Doehring 2006, pp.74–77):

- material – extrinsic things, but may well have an intrinsic meaning too that connects with someone, somewhere or something that is personally significant

- relational – lost opportunities for intimacy, whether psychological, physical, spiritual and so on

- intrapsychic – loss of an ideal or symbol, such as becoming a sibling

- functional – losing a function of the body with varying degrees of disability and dependence

- role – loss of a role that may happen at transition such as death and that can also be experienced when a contract or agreement or stage of life comes to an end

- systemic – change in family, faith or other organisational system that means it functions in a different way.

When we think about losses experienced and felt by children, they can be around loss of feeling safe, security, feeling loved and cared for, significant people, abilities, position, status, self-image or self-esteem. Perhaps some of those you relate to don't call this loss, as it is all they have known. What is most important to acknowledge is that a child can and will feel significant loss that has nothing to do with physical death or bereavement. However, bereavement theory can offer some helpful insights as to what a child may be experiencing (see Table 2.1):

TABLE 2.1: STAGES OF BEREAVEMENT

Phase	Kübler-Ross 2009	Bowlby and Parkes 1970
1	Denial	Numbness
2	Rage, anger, bargaining, depression	Pining Disorganisation
3	Acceptance	Re-organisation

These stages are helpful for us to be prepared for and normalise particular responses to loss. The critique of this stages model is that it can be linear, that we go through each step in a certain direction, even for a set amount of time, but this is not necessarily a fair interpretation. The responses to loss and expressions of grief are not that systematic, but rather, individual and dynamic. I find a more helpful model is the waterfall and whirlpool (Wilson 1993), where the river of life can be going along calmly and then the sudden tragedies and losses of life can plunge us into places and times of grief and uncertainty. Then we have the normality of the river for a while, until we feel like we are falling off the end of the world again, and so it goes on over days, weeks, months and even years.

Children handling sorrow

In working with children it can be helpful to remember that:

> the one thing we can say about childhood therefore, is that it is a time of enormous change. Nothing stays the same for very long, which means that children are often better able than adults to deal with change, because they are experiencing it all the time. (Drane and Drane 2009, pp.216–217)

However, it may sometimes need some skilled intervention to help a child overcome sorrow through their loss. There may be all sorts of reasons that children find it difficult to talk about their sorrow, and one of the things that we have found helpful is doing a child-friendly version of the examen. Here a child decorates a wooden lolly stick figure with one side having a happy face and the other a sad face. At the end of each day or weekly, for example, go through this with them, asking when they have been happy and when they have been sad. They can write the questions on the stick: When was I happiest? When was I saddest?

Bereavement

It is difficult in such a short space here to go into all the ways different aged children respond to grief. What I hope will be helpful is a list of issues and questions that will need to be taken into account when supporting bereaved children:

- What do they understand 'dead' to mean? Cannot move, separation, there is a reason they died, everything dies at some point, they are not in pain any more, they will look different...(adapted from Edwards and Titman 2010, p.159).

- It is okay to be very sad and upset. Other people are as well.

- Questions children may have about a deceased person: when will they wake up? When will I see them again?

One of the projects I was involved in was to produce some Christian resources to support children at end of life and in bereavement. The book for siblings is called *Jesus Still Loves Joe* (Beech and PCN 2011), and it emphasises how it is alright to experience lots of sometimes-difficult emotions (it is also available as an online video[1]).

---

1   www.paediatric-chaplaincy-network.org/media/online-videos/jesus-still-loves-joe

Multiple losses/grief

An important insight around loss theory is to do with the concept and experience of multiple loss, of the same or different losses in close proximity to each other. This explains why some of us lose the plot over the most trivial thing, because it reflects the 'straw that broke the camel's back', and it is an accumulation of loss. This may lead to either complex grief or psychological grief, which are technical terms for when grief is being expressed either unhealthily or over a prolonged length of time without much sense of moving on. Interestingly with illness, as we found in some research we did with young people with cancer (Darby, Nash and Nash 2014), there can be a sense of anticipatory grief, imagining what is to come.

Within a spectrum we can understand that much grief is normal but complex. Why would children know how to understand loss and grief for the first time? Such powerful emotions are hard enough for adults, and sometimes we may not have prepared children for a loss that we know is coming, or we may not model healthy ways of sharing when we feel sad.

Bullying

Bullying happens when targeted aggression happens; it can be one-on-one, group-on-one or group-on-group. It is often the result of an oppressive use of power and may be linked to prejudice, discrimination or stereotyping. Children are bullied for a variety of reasons including appearance, dress, disability or physical difference, gender, sexuality, lack of confidence, ethnicity, class, geography, interests and so on. Bullying encompasses a wide range of behaviours with one of the current discussions being what the difference is between banter and bullying. It is easy to try to dismiss bullying behaviour by saying that it was just a bit of banter, but it can feel devastating to a child, as this poem shows:

> Sticks and stones may break my bones, but words can also hurt me.
> Sticks and stones break only skin, while words are ghosts that haunt me...
> Pain from words has left its scar, on mind and heart that's tender.
> Cuts and bruises now have healed, it's words that I remember.[2]

Bullying may also take the form of physical attack or 'jokes', spreading rumours, gossip, exclusion or harassment, and this can now take place online or face to face. The prevalence of children with smartphones means that the reach of the bully can be everywhere, all the time.

2   See www.poemhunter.com/poem/sticks-and-stones-10

Statistics suggest that nearly half of children are bullied at some point in their time at school.[3] Research (Brown, Clery and Ferguson 2011) suggests that over 16,000 children are absent from state schools in the UK due to bullying, and it is the most common reason for children under 11 contacting Childline (NSPCC 2016). It is clearly a serious problem and one where, as the NSPCC found, some children are afraid to speak out because they think it may make matters worse while others say you should stand up to bullies. The support of adults is often needed.

Discernment

Prayerful wisdom is needed in knowing how to respond to bullying. Even with all the research that has been done, there is no definitive reason as to why it happens, but there are contributory factors. When a dual-heritage child is referred to as 'chocolate' or a child is consciously victimised online for being good at school, it is important to understand what motivates such behaviour. Maliciousness, ignorance of effect, over-stepping/enthusiastic play, repeated behaviour, retaliation, acting out, awkward expression of growing in confidence, seeking power and control are just some of the reasons it may happen. I am not seeking to justify the behaviour, but attempting to first understand why it happens, in order to be most effective in dealing with it.

Although our hearts go out to those who are bullied, those who bully have many negative reasons for doing so, and many do not go on to lead flourishing lives either. Many experts now feel that bullying is a learned behaviour: 'too little love and too much rejection' (CQ Researcher 2012, p.145). We are very likely to be dealing with both the child doing the bullying as well as the one being bullied in our ministry.

The forgotten parties

Bystanders, those who observe bullying, are an often-forgotten group of children in this discussion. They, too, can be supported to speak up. Telling tales is a mentality that is difficult to break out of, but stressing community responsibility and caring for others will appeal, and will motivate other children to appropriately report. The bully will also have their helpers and supporters.

---

3   See the Anti-Bullying Alliance at www.anti-bullyingalliance.org.uk

Anti-bullying programmes

Programmes that work tend to be those that are proactive, preventative and provide a safe place and opportunity for all those involved, both the bully and the bullied (Lindon 2012). Other elements are:

- shared responsibility within the context

- improving the self-esteem of both parties

- teaching assertive body language: upright posture, dismissive shrugs, walking proudly away

- helping move aggression to assertive behaviour for the bully

- helping build friendships for the bullied

- encouraging and facilitating safe reporting: buddy systems, peer reporting, adverts

- systemic non-tolerance policy and practice: non-trivialised, un-acceptable behaviour

- restorative justice, facilitated meetings between parties.

As Lindon notes, 'When children have a secure sense of belonging then their sense of self-esteem need not be at the cost of undermining other people' (2012, p.64).

Transition

A transition is a change from one thing to the next. Between schools is the most common time and type of transition, but there are many others. These are some of the main different types and times of transitions:

- age/child/adolescent/adult/development stages

- schooling

- children to adult institutions, for example, hospital

- health to illness

- cared-for to carer

- wealth to poverty

- home to homelessness

- integrated to fragmented family.

Transition can be both liberating and joyful, but also threatening and scary. Whatever the context, preparation is generally acknowledged as key: to start discussions, visit early, to raise awareness, to encourage questions. Most transition is difficult because it involves change, moving on from the known into the unknown. Children are doing this within their normative emotional, physical and cognitive development, which is hard enough anyway. Individual support is also necessary because children are so different and their pressure points will vary. At the age of 16, Petra,[4] one of our Birmingham Children's Hospital patients on dialysis, was introduced to the adult unit at her local general hospital where she would be gradually transitioned to. It was all done very well, but she went from being the oldest, most well-known patient in a child-centred unit to being one of many in an age-diverse unit, sitting for four hours three times a week with older adults and without some of the additional support you get in a paediatric hospital from chaplains, youth and play workers.

Safeguarding

The UK government has developed the policy and practice of safeguarding from its previous approach of child protection, and churches will usually have these policies in place and increasingly a robust system of training for people involved in work with children and young people. Safeguarding involves:

- protecting children from maltreatment

- preventing the impairment of children's health and development

- ensuring that children grow up in circumstances consistent with the provision of safe and effective care

- taking action to enable all children to have the best outcomes.[5]

One of the key perspectives of safeguarding is that policies are in place for the safety of everyone. I find the ethical spectrum of rights and responsibilities helpful in not just keeping the letter of the law but also being motivated to look out for everyone involved in my children's work. Thus I have on my radar the rights and responsibilities of the children, the family, the leaders and the immediate and wider communities to which we belong. Any pastoral care should be offered within the boundaries of

---

4   All names have been anonymised.
5   See www.gov.uk/government/publications/safeguarding-children-and-young-people/ safeguarding-children-and-young-people

your local safeguarding policy, and all those who are involved in work with children and young people should receive safeguarding training. Denominations have good practice guidelines around this area, including for the recruitment of volunteers. We need to be aware that 'Many children face risks and harms that can be barriers to reaching their potential, and for some children these risks are far more numerous and far higher than for others' (Masson 2009, p.160).

Introduction to key principles

So what might pastoral care and support look and feel like for children in these kinds of situations?

Providing a safe place

Essential to these principles is creating a safe place for children to flourish during difficult times. Play and ritual may be significant in this as they can help in voicing and naming feelings. Pearmain (2005), although talking specifically about summer camps, uses the term 'safe haven' to describe what is created. She sees three things as important in this that might inform the way we structure our work with children (2005, p.281):

Significant threshold aspects:

- profound experience of welcome and inclusion

- sustained experience of acceptance

- no judgements.

Significant opportunities for feeling free and safe:

- opportunities for sharing in small groups

- fun and games

- spiritual space for reflection, integration, depth of being, connection

- sense of freedom and spontaneous expression encouraged.

Significant community structures:

- firm ground rules

- shared values

- consistency of structure

- sense of belonging in a group/community.

Duty of care and helping build resilience

A duty of care is the responsibility an organisation has when an in *loco parentis* is concerned with the safety and wellbeing of a child. Resilience involves building up internal resources to help a child cope with situations that occur, helping them to become stronger or bounce back after experiencing difficult situations. While this might seem very obvious, I propose that many of us have a default, that if we are left to our own devices in children's pastoral care, we will care for a child within an inch of every boundary going, or we will endorse their existing ability to rise above their current difficult situation. The Church and Christian organisations have a responsibility for both with children.

Danger: Not either/or but both

In supporting children we need to ensure our programmes and projects do both. There is a current move towards building resilience, but the concern and critique of this is that building resilience puts the onus on the child, that it is their responsibility to do, to be something, that it's on them. My concern is that it can distract away from our duty of care to provide what we are responsible for, which is to provide a place that:

- provides a safe, welcoming, affirming environment

- offers a supportive environment to process difficult experiences

- understands that individuals may develop at different speeds and have different needs.

Pastoral care with integrity

This involves the basics of being fully present and available, active listening and watching, paying attention, permission to be honest about one's self, and being non-judgemental.

I SEE YOU

I love this term; one of its roots is from the African Zulu greeting, Sawubona. It is more than hello. It means to acknowledge that someone is there, that they exist, they are important and significant enough to be noticed – this is how I want every child I meet to feel. This involves eye contact, taking time to lean down or get on their level; my 100 per cent focus is for that moment on them.

MAKING A CONNECTION

This is at the essence of our spiritual as well as pastoral wellbeing, that a connection is available, made and felt. This is important between the child and a significant adult, God, other children and the wider Church (as well as family).

Ask children where and what is best for them to feel safe to talk. We are not seeking to make a child talk, disclose or reveal if that is not what they want to do; rather, we are creating a safe conducive place for them to do so should they wish. We might think it could be for their best if they did, but unless it is about abuse, to push them is to disrespect their autonomy.

Referrals

We also need to be aware that there are times when we will need to make a referral, as what the child needs pastorally is beyond our competence or experience. It is important to always talk this through and to remain available to the child as well as being willing to accompany them if that is what they would like.

Permission and prayers

We should always get permission from the child before sharing a child's need, or invite the child themselves to share with the group so they control the information being given. We might even want to consider permission from the parent before certain needs are shared.

Assume we don't know or understand

There is always so much going on within and without a child that it would be naive and possibly an insult to assume we really know them and understand all that is going on for them. We don't want to communicate a lack of confidence in our ability to engage, but we do want to make it clear that they can say anything they want to and we are not prejudging or making assumptions or jumping to conclusions.

Improving communication and making connections

Our objective is to ensure communication happens and keeps happening. Although the writers of the following list are writing about bereavement, it has universal usage for all our themes. Edwards and Titman (2010) suggest that we:

- follow the cues from the children

- show the child that you appreciate their thoughts and questions and take them seriously

- answer the children's questions in a straightforward, honest and reassuring way

- always check that the child already knows or thinks about what they have asked you

- create opportunities for children to communicate in a variety of ways, including play, pictures, poetry and stories

- ensure that all adults caring for the child are in good communication about what the children have been told, to ensure consistent information

- give children the opportunity to revisit this conversation and build their knowledge over time.

Other helpful skills and approaches are to reflect back or ask clarifying questions:

- 'Did I hear you say…?'

- 'That's interesting. Can I ask you what you mean by that?'

- 'Would you like me to put that another way?'

Calling it how it is may also be appropriate. Affirming children's feelings, communicating that they have been heard, is a wonderful gift to offer to children. For example, saying 'Oh, that sounds horrible' at the right time may well encourage the child to become even more open with us or to clam up if they think we cannot take any more. Much of what we say is a judgement call based on who we are, the child we are with and the topic of conversation. They can offer us a little test and we can pass with flying colours or fail, and we may not always know that this is what they were doing.

It is also helpful to make a note of anniversaries. The great thing about electronic diaries is that we can do yearly reminders. With my dyslexia, I would not even remember the anniversary of the death of my own mother!

Assessment and care plans where appropriate

This question constantly challenges me: 'Why do some children emerge from a highly stressful and harmful situation psychologically intact, while others are subject to significantly less adversity and cope much less effectively?' (Keenan, Evans and Crowley 2016, p.352). Sometimes we need to have a more purposeful approach to learn from those who are doing well, but also to ensure we have proper support in place for those who are struggling. In my children's hospital context the idea of assessment and care plans is the norm, and perhaps we need to think about being more purposeful sometimes in our ministry setting too. Some of the headings I would use to reflect on or record include:

- emotional: issues, depth, impact

- cognitive: how do they understand what has happened?

- physical: harm, illness, signs

- behavioural: changes, unhealthy, normal behaviour

- relational: who do they best/least relate to?

- faith and spiritual: growing faith.

This spectrum would give us a comprehensive holistic list of the effects the issue is having on the child. By exploring these categories, it will enable us to draw on different child development theories such as Piaget (cognitive, social, moral), Vygotsky (cognitive, intellectual), Bowlby (relational), Kohlberg (moral), Gardner (emotional), Myers–Briggs (personality and temperament), or Fowler and Westerhoff (faith and spiritual) (for an accessible introduction to these major theorists, see Bennett 2016).

Do some preparatory work

Let's not just wait to manage a crisis when it occurs; let's be proactive in the meantime. We have much more chance of doing considered non-knee-jerk ministry if we have critical incident plans where this is appropriate in the way that institutions do. For example, you may want to offer support to a local school as part of their critical incident plan, should a situation occur.

Interventions

Planning interventions, responses to disclosed or identified needs, is what we do all the time. Calling them interventions gives them an intentionality, a plan for a desired outcome. This could be one-to-one or group work, around targeted themes or issues that we have identified, and often with the children themselves contributing.

Consider:

- having a recording system and sheet for a child where this is appropriate; this will need to been kept in a secure locked place in accordance with your data protection policy

- having a critical incident policy including preparing some activities for when a child comes to you in loss

- having a code of conduct and anti-bullying policy in place that is designed with the help of the children

- having an early intervention approach.

Work with the family

In the hospital context it is usual practice to do nothing with children that we have not already been given permission to do by parents/carers. Churches will usually have consent forms for everyday activities as well as for trips or residentials.

Confidentiality

This is always going to be difficult, but the general principle of 'I will only tell someone else if I think you are going to harm yourself or others' usually holds. When it comes to disclosures covered by your safeguarding policy, you need to be clear with the child what you need to do. Many of us have found that it is best to be upfront if asked or even be clear before you sense a major discussion is going to start. It is worth taking this risk even if you think the child may not tell you anything else, because the child is then informed in advance of potential outcomes. If the referral or request comes from a parent to support their child, it is again best to be clear about their expectations of what the parent will be told and what feedback is expected. Agreeing phrases like 'Do you mind if I tell mummy or daddy this?' need to be asked to ensure collusion is not happening. At times we need to courageously and with wisdom challenge and work towards the place where the family and the child all know what it is that others know.

Name and celebrate assets

It is easy to concentrate on what the child does not have, has lost or would like, but it is also important to name and celebrate what the child does have. Even when we are in our lowest place, we still have inner and external resources to support us and keep us going.

TRY IT

Think of a time when you felt most sad, upset, grieved or worried. What you did not have most easily comes to mind, but think about the people, inner attitudes, resources or skills that you did have to keep going. The objective is not to dismiss how bad and/or sad the current situation is; we are not seeking to be trite about how difficult life might be, but to compliment the child that they have more than that which they have lost, fear, and so on.

Spiritual intelligence

Building on the work of Gardner's multiple intelligence, Sinetar (2000) uses the term 'early awakeners' for young children who have this. She suggests the qualities of spiritually intelligent children include:

- acute self-awareness

- broad worldview

- moral elevation, strong opinions, a tendency to experience delight

- an understanding of where they are headed

- unappeasable hunger for selected interests

- fresh weird notions, a well developed sense of humour

- pragmatic, efficient perceptions of reality.

I recognised many of these in Dani. We have a book of blob pictures,[6] and I was looking to do one of them with Dani. However, she had a different idea. She took the book off of me and flicked through every page, commenting on where she saw herself in the picture. When she got to blob family, she matter-of-factly just turned the page over, saying 'I don't have one of those.' Despite what on the outside looked like a very complex situation, she manifested many of these characteristics of a spiritually intelligent child.

---

6 See www.pipwilson.com

We have an activity we often use in an initial encounter with patients at Birmingham Children's Hospital. For shorthand we call it the 'bead bracelet', and we encourage patients to make a bracelet with different coloured beads that represent different things such as peace, self-worth, honesty, happiness, belonging. We encourage them to do the bracelet in two halves: things they bring with them to hospital and things they need in hospital (for details, see Nash, Darby and Nash 2015, pp.186–188). We end up with some profound conversations about spiritual issues and their own spirituality.

Create intentional opportunities for play and exploration

Play is understood to be the natural world of children, and it is an obvious place for us to implement a safe place for children to acknowledge, articulate and reveal their feelings. 'Play allows children to use their creativity while developing their imagination, dexterity, and physical, cognitive, and emotion strength. Play is freely chosen personally directed, intrinsically motivated behaviour that actively engages the child' (O'Connell 2013, p.52).

Support our teams: Self-care

Most of the issues and work described in this chapter are difficult issues to engage with, and draining upon those involved in supporting children and their families. We also have a duty of care for our leaders, to ensure they are and feel safe to respond. This can mean having proper debrief sessions, and doing a training audit to see what the team feel confident and competent in dealing with.

Having a theological basis and rationale for our care in difficult situations

It has been said if you can do theology by the bedside of a dying child, you can do theology anywhere. I would certainly say that working out my understanding of God and the work of the Kingdom in a children's hospital has given me some transferable insights for other contexts (see Nash 2011). So what within our faith helps us make sense of and supports us in our care of children?

Unconditional love

This will be the base line and highest pinnacle of how we relate and treat the children we support. Chapman and Campbell (2016) talk about the five love languages of children, and suggest that each child has a preferred love language. The five are:

- quality time

- words of affirmation

- gifts

- acts of service

- physical touch (in line with good safeguarding practice).

If we are aware of a child's preference, then our care and support can be more effective and bespoke for them. If our love can manifest itself in such a way as these, to find out from each child how they prefer to be loved through these stressful times, our care and support will surely be more bespoke to every child we care for. I also like the idea of understanding love by offering every child unconditional positive regard (Rogers 1956); this captures the essence of grace.

We have a redemptive faith

What I find sustaining in our faith is that at the heart of our salvation is a redeeming God, a God who can and desires to bring good from negative situations. One of the greatest aspects of redemption is that although good can come out of bad situations, we still get to call the harm, sin, grieved against, bad. Just because a child grows in confidence, this does not mean that the bully did them a favour! Our God is able to bring so much good out of a negative or wrong situation that we can be tempted to believe God planned for it to happen. Please let us avoid this temptation, and not border on justification of harm.

We work out our faith in the liminal, the in-between places

This type of care is reaching out to the margins of our mission. We are seeking to support those whose lives have become messy and sad in the pressures of everyday living in our troubled and beautiful world.

We lament with those who are sad and weep

We have a compassionate faith and mission that respond to sadness, not with trite answers, but meeting sadness with sadness. To acknowledge the circumstances of our children is not to have a lack of faith but dignifies their experiences and feelings. 'I am so sorry for your loss' is sometimes all that I feel is appropriate on being in the room with a very recently bereaved family. Every time the New Testament speaks about rejoicing in suffering, it is referring to being persecuted for our faith, not being glad we are bullied for being who we are or sad that my dad died, for example.

Holy indignation and righteous rage

Because we are a people who pray for God's Kingdom to come on earth as it is in Heaven, desiring and working for justice is part of what we do. We can have a righteous anger in the light of and response to unrighteous oppression towards those who cannot fend for themselves. Parker suggests that:

> ...black adolescent rage, when the Holy Spirit works through that rage, has power to save humankind from sin, which includes race, class and gender injustice. When black adolescent rage is placed in God's redeeming embrace, known in Jesus Christ, it has the power to transform those sins that denigrates and dehumanize all our sisters and brothers, regardless of age, race, and ethnicity, socioeconomic status, or sexuality. This redemptive rage is *holy indignation*. (2008, p.207; original emphasis)

Choosing to forgive

I am always inspired by families who have had a family member murdered or killed when they consciously choose to forgive the perpetrator. They choose the hard road, not of revenge and bitterness, but of forgiveness and healing. Encouraging our children to take this path is sometimes a difficult one, but I am convinced that it is one that leads to healing and righteousness, even in the face of justifiable anger. It is an integral part of the Gospel message.

Presence

This is what we get to role-model – walking with God, and seeking to express our faith during difficult times. We can even hope that if our children get to do theology, faith-seeking understanding, during the difficult times of their lives this will, in turn, sustain them and encourage them as they grow older, that their God is relevant, faithful and worthy of their devotion. As Mother Teresa said as she sought to work out her faith in places of lament, in need of redemption and justice, she found Jesus in distressing disguises.

Conclusion

These times may be critical in a child's faith development, spiritual and emotional wellbeing and formation. These times may well have been traumatic or disturbing, and the child may have felt out of control with few resources to handle them. Our support during these times can be the difference between a child flourishing or floundering. White (2011) argues that there are five essential elements that we need to offer if love is to help a child grow: security, boundaries, significance, community, and creativity. When we seek to offer a normative environment in our children's work of creating space and opportunities to ask, explore, create, be quiet and still, when we model honesty, reassurance, expecting the unexpected, nurture memories and inform, discuss and refer as necessary, then hopefully our children will rarely need rescuing, But they do need and deserve an affirmation of their being loved and held by God and by us. Then we will have created a place and a type of children's work that is safe for disclosures from the darkness into the light.

> ### QUESTIONS FOR REFLECTION AND DISCUSSION
>
> - How do you create space for children to share things that are troubling them?
>
> - In what ways do you help children manage different transitions in their lives?
>
> - Which theological perspectives help you to process some of the difficult pastoral encounters you have?
>
> - What are the principles that underpin your approach to pastoral care?
>
> - Are there any training needs or changes in practice you want to consider as a consequence of reading this chapter?

References and further reading

Beech, V. and PCN (Paediatric Chaplaincy Network) (2011) *Jesus still loves Joe*. Birmingham: Christian Education. [Video available at www.paediatric-chaplaincy-network.org/media/online-videos]

Bennett, C. (2016) *Growing Upwards: The Faith Journey of Christian Young People*. Cambridge: Grove Youth Series, Y44.

Borgman, D. (2003) *Hear My Story*. Peabody, MA: Hendrickson.

Bowlby, J. and Parkes, C.M. (1970) 'Separation and loss within the family.' *The Child in His Family 1*, 197–216.

Brown, V., Clery, E. and Ferguson, C. (2011) 'Estimating the prevalence of young people absent from school due to bullying.' *National Centre for Social Research 1*, 1–61.

Chapman, G.D. and Campbell, R. (2016) *The 5 Love Languages of Children*. Chicago, IL: Moody Publishers.

CQ Researcher (2012) *Children and Adolescence in Society*. London: Sage.

Darby, K., Nash, P. and Nash, S. (2014) 'Understanding and responding to spiritual and religious needs of young people with cancer: Kathryn Darby and colleagues explore ways to support this patient group by focusing on non-medical aspects of care.' *Cancer Nursing Practice 13*(2), 32–37.

Doehring, C. (2006) *The Practice of Pastoral Care*. Louisville, KY: Westminster John Knox.

Drane, J. and Drane, O.M.F. (2009) 'Death.' In A. Richards and P. Privett (eds) *Through the Eyes of a Child* (pp. 205–222). London: Church House Publishing.

Edwards, M. and Titman, P. (2010) *Promoting Psychological Well-being in Children with Acute and Chronic Illness*. London: Jessica Kingsley Publishers.

Keenan, T., Evans, S. and Crowley, K. (2016) *An Introduction to Child Development*. London: Sage.

Kübler-Ross, E. (2009) *On Death and Dying: What the Dying Have to Teach Doctors, Nurses, Clergy and Their Own Families*. London: Taylor & Francis.

Lindon, J. (2012) *Understanding Children's Behaviour 0–11*. London: Hodder Education.

Masson, J. (2009) 'Child Protection.' In H. Montgomery and M. Kellett (eds) *Children and Young People's Worlds* (pp.145–164). Bristol: Policy Press.

Nash, P. (2011) *Supporting Dying Children and Their Families*. London: SPCK.

Nash, P., Bartel, M. and Nash, S. (2018) *Paediatric Chaplaincy*. London: Jessica Kingsley Publishers.

Nash, P., Darby, K. and Nash, S. (2015) *Spiritual Care with Sick Children and Young People*. London: Jessica Kingsley Publishers.

NSPCC (2016) *What Children Are Telling Us about Bullying: The Experiences of Young People Contacting Childline about Bullying in 2015/16*. Available at www.nspcc.org.uk/services-and-resources/research-and-resources/2016/what-children-are-telling-us-about-bullying

O'Connell, D. (2013) *Working with Children and Young People – Good Practice Guidelines for Healthcare Chaplains*. Birmingham: Red Balloon Resources.

Parker, E. (2008) 'Sanctified Rage.' In M.E. Moore and A.M. Wright (eds) *Children, Youth and Spirituality in a Troubling World* (pp.196–209). St Louis, MO: Chalice Press.

Pearmain, R. (2005) 'Transformational experiences in young people: The meaning of a safe haven.' *International Journal of Children's Spirituality 10*(3), 277–290.

Rogers, C. (1956) *Client-centered Therapy* (3rd edn). Boston, MA: Houghton-Mifflin.

Sinetar, M. (2000) *Spiritual Intelligence*. Maryknoll, NY: Orbis Books.

White, K. (2011) *The Growth of Love*. Abingdon: Barnabas.

Wilson, R. (1993) 'Bereavement care – The role of the paediatrician.' *Current Paediatrics 3*(2), 86–91.

Chapter 3

FACEBOOK FRIEND

Socialisation, Socialising and Social Networking

Carolyn Edwards

Introduction

This chapter explores the nature of the network of relationships that surround children in their growth and learning. Using the metaphor of 'Facebook friend', it investigates the challenges and opportunities present for children and children's workers in a variety of social connections, and how we can best nurture children in healthy connections and relationships in twenty-first-century family and community life.

When considering children's spirituality and faith development it is important to understand the current cultural context that children are living in. There is an ancient African phrase that says 'it takes a village to raise a child'. Sometimes as I watch families out and about, sitting in coffee shops, waiting rooms and bus stops, I wonder if, in the twenty-first century, we have fallen into the trap of believing that it takes a screen to raise a child. Children, as a sociological category, might be healthier and safer now than they have ever been in history, but the 2017 *Good Childhood Report* cites emotional neglect as a key factor in what is for many not a 'good' childhood.

Human beings have a deep-seated need for connection. We are made in the image of a Trinitarian God. Theologians use the term 'perichoresis' formed from the Greek words 'peri', which means 'around', and 'chorein', which means 'make room', to help us understand the nature of that trinity. Indicated in passages like John 17.1 and John 16.14, perichoresis is often translated to mean 'rotation' or 'a going around', and expresses the relationship of the Godhead as one of constant reciprocity and preferment of other, based on true intimacy and love. While this level of harmony might be beyond our human understanding, it is an aspiration of our DNA and something which, I believe, we long for and strive to achieve. What's more, as Christakis and Fowler (2011) suggest in their book *Connected*, our social connections have an impact on every area of our daily living.

My academic research on children's spirituality and years of experience in the field has led me to believe that for healthy spirituality and mental wellbeing, children need to experience four types of connection: a connection with God; a connection with other people; a connection with themselves; and a connection with the world around them. These need to be deep connections that involve a sense of belonging, awe and wonder, meaning-making and purpose, and that take time and intentional investment to enhance. Due to the work of writers like Bowlby and Ainsworth we now know how important a child forming a secure attachment to primary carers in infancy is for healthy emotional development. Writers on faith development like Fowler and Westerhoff also stress the importance of trust and relationships as the foundation of faith, with both citing 'belonging' as an elementary stage in faith development. How we connect with others is crucial, and our job, as those who are alongside children, is to help them form connections that are healthy and enhancing, not limited and limiting.

One of the social connections prevalent today is social media, hence the title for this chapter. It's a way that we can feel more connected with the people we love or have just met once, wish we saw more of, or wish we didn't know what they had for tea every day! Recent statistics suggest that 60 per cent of the adult population of the UK is using social media and 23 per cent of eight- to eleven-year-olds (for further information, read the media usage reports by Ofcom[1]). Online connection is a way of life, but what is the impact that it is having on our children, how they connect with the world, and how we connect with them? Using some of the positive and negative elements of an online connection – a Facebook friend – in this chapter I explore children's connectivity in the twenty-first century, and provide some recommendations as to what we can do in response.

A Facebook friend is a much-needed social connection

In their book *Connected*, Christakis and Fowler (2011) discuss the power of social networks and the science behind them. They suggest that social connections and networks are important and powerful, and question

---

1   https://www.ofcom.org.uk/research-and-data/media-literacy-research/adults/
    adults-media-use-and-attitudes

where the altruism often needed to maintain them has evolved from. They argue that the prevailing understanding of humanity – where in a 'dog-eat-dog' world our species relies on self-interest to get the best for ourselves, perhaps at the expense of others – should be replaced with 'network person', where our connection with others has allowed us to evolve the ability to care about others and take their wellbeing into account. The research they cite to build this argument was all carried out with adults, but I think similar research done among children gives us some helpful insights into how we are wired altruistically. Using stickers as the resource in research carried out with pre-schoolers, Moore (2009) concluded that there is a biological programming for behaviour that causes young children to divide fairly what they have, not only with their friends, but also with children who are strangers to them. But Moore is viewing this phenomenon from a secular perspective, and I think it is more than that. This is humanity, made in the image of the Trinitarian God of perichoresis, even in its earliest stages of socialisation, reflecting some of the model of reciprocity and preferment of other, simply because that is how we are wired.

Children encounter all sorts of people in their daily lives, at pre-school or school, in the shops and library, and at home. One of the downsides of the need to protect children from those with predatory intent is that these natural connections and potential relationships are being eroded.

The man who lives across the road from the school, and who waves at the children as they arrive and leave every day, may simply be reminded of his own now grown-up children or geographically distant grandchildren, and yet now maybe he watches from behind a closed curtain, his joy curtailed by the fear of mistrust and glares from worried mothers – the children missing out on the daily reminder of their importance. The woman who naturally talks to anyone thinks twice before chatting to the child next to her in the queue, and so the child misses out on the opportunity to share the deep thought they just had about the pavement they are standing on. The school worker caught in their costume and towel at the swimming pool scuttles into the changing room rather than hearing how much of the story they told in assembly last week that child can remember.

Church is one of the few places that children can meet adults of all shapes and sizes safely. Of course, we need to make sure that we adhere to safeguarding policies and guidelines, but we also need to find ways to encourage social connections that are fun and rewarding for all generations, and socialise children for a variety of independent connections when they are older. In *Connected* the authors suggest that higher 'happiness' is recorded for those with greater 'transivity'. By this they mean the number of connections there are between their loved ones and each other. So, if my good friend also knows one of my other friends well, my transivity is increased, and this positively affects my emotional wellbeing. This, I believe, has an important impact on a child's sense of belonging in the Church. If a child is only connected with the other eight- to eleven-year-olds through junior church, then when those children leave, for whatever reason, that child's connectivity reduces dramatically, and it is highly likely that they will leave and their faith be negatively impacted. If, however, the child is connected with a variety of adults in the Church, through intergenerational activity and intentional investment from the adults, then not only will the child feel more connected and more likely to stay, but the high transivity in the congregation is also likely to have a positive attitude on their emotional wellbeing.

In our risk-averse culture, where parents are not allowing children and young people to play outside or meet up and 'hang out', digital media can also offer a positive avenue for social connectivity, a place where they can 'hang out'. Other research suggests that a large proportion of teenage digital communication is concerned with making arrangements to meet up with friends in person, and that social and digital media can augment social connectivity rather than limit it; it is just doing it in a way that few adults understand (boyd 2008). For children, games like Minecraft® have created community and the opportunity for social interaction in an environment that is simple and lacks the need to interpret and communicate with intricate social cues. This might be a good thing for a child who feels socially isolated, and it has been argued that parents do not need to worry that their children are spending hours absorbed in the game, as not only is it engaging their imaginations, but it is also giving them opportunities to develop offline social skills online. I am not completely convinced, however, as many online social connections can remain superficial.

A Facebook friend is not an emotionally deep connection

For many years research on the impact online activity is having on children has been inconclusive, with some writers arguing that media use might provide social cohesion for children with the same interests, particularly boys (Heim *et al.* 2007). More recently, insights from neuroscience have led child psychologists to express concern about the potential impact online engagement, particularly via phones and tablets, has on children's emotional development. As infants' brains develop, there is a surge of neural growth at about three years of age. This is when children really start to develop what is called 'theory of mind' – the ability to differentiate one's own perspective and preferences from someone else's. It is also the stage where they start to develop empathy and make friends. This happens as neural pathways are burned and connections made. Extended time on phones and tablets, it is suggested, get in the way of this development. In addition, eyes on a screen, rather than on other humans in the vicinity, whether at a meal table or in a play space, mean that a child's ability to learn social cues, and how to compromise and negotiate, is also inhibited. I recently heard a radio presenter talk about the length of time an adult can bear whining from the back of a car on a long journey before they hand over their phone. Unwittingly they were revealing the dopamine addiction caused by extended screen time that then results in an inability to regulate emotion. As the child engages with the screen, because it is a pleasurable activity, the hormone dopamine is released and the child is soothed, the neural pathway that is stimulated naturally wants more of this, so the child needs more screen time to be soothed. If this pattern is cultivated during the difficult period when the child is developing the ability to self-soothe (techniques can range from thumb sucking to talking to pets or toys) and regulate their own emotions (taught and modelled by a boundaried relationship with a primary carer), then there is a high likelihood, as the radio presenter bemoaned, that the screen becomes the only thing that will calm and placate the child.

A Facebook friend is a source of identity formation and affirmation

Watch any child engaging with cars, trains and pretend play, and it is easy to see that as humans we not only pass goods and services through networks, but also social and moral norms. Christakis and Fowler (2011) refer to these as 'contagion', and perhaps less expectedly, suggest that we also pass emotions, referring to several extreme cases of epidemic hysteria spread through social connections. We have probably all met an adult who now refuses to engage with the Christian faith because when they were a child it 'felt' boring, judgemental and miserable. Children pick up on emotions, and I would argue are particularly susceptible to 'contagions' that are passed through their social connections. Children who 'feel' loved in Church are more likely to stay, than those who 'feel' that those around them are unhappy, but in addition, we need to consider what other 'contagions' we are passing through our connections.

These can be 'goods and services' such as entertaining programmes and biblical truths, but just as importantly, feelings of acceptance and a deep-seated understanding of grace and what it looks like in real life.

As children move through infancy, childhood and adolescence into adulthood, they are striving to obtain autonomy in their identity – autonomy being an active process located in the physical, psychosocial, cognitive and moral, and I would argue, spiritual domains, whereby an individual develops towards independence and personal freedom. Various studies indicate that digital media and the internet serve as a 'playground' in which young people can experiment with their identity (Gross 2005). This could be considered both a positive and a negative factor, but also means that children can be exposed to unhealthy contagion that parents and carers are unaware of. Certainly, I think many feel ineffective, and many are oblivious to the impact that overtly sexual material that is part of much multi-media content (for instance, pop music videos) is having on children's identity formation.

Children learn by looking and watching non-verbal clues. Social media icons are an easy way of knowing whether others approve of, or like, or are entertained by, what you have posted. Face-to-face communication might be harder to discern. We might instinctively know how to communicate with children in ways that affirm their presence and worth: by crouching down when they talk so that we are eye to eye; smiling and nodding to demonstrate that we are listening; and asking questions that show that we remember other things that they have shared with us. How can we encourage, affirm and facilitate other members of the congregation to participate in nurturing the spirituality and faith of the children present in these ways, creating positive contagion?

A Facebook friend can be a source of anxiety, jealousy and low self-esteem

Research carried out by Pea and colleagues with 191 eight- to-twelve-year-olds in the US reported a series of negative socio-emotional outcomes associated with media multi-tasking (Pea et al. 2012). These included: feeling less social success, not feeling normal, having more friends whom parents perceive as a bad influence, and sleeping less. Conversely, face-to-face communication was strongly associated with positive social wellbeing. They suggest that the growth of media multi-tasking should be viewed with some concern (Pea et al. 2012), particularly because it is in late childhood and early adolescence that children are increasingly conscious of how others perceive them and they are still learning emotional expression and interpretation for social interaction. Peer social success has been identified as one of the three major dimensions of competence in child/adolescent development, and therefore Pea *et al.*'s research raises concerns.

Without space and time to 'wonder' and consider alternative models of 'being' it is less likely that humanity realises its fulfilling sense of self. For children and young people who have less 'down time', there is therefore a risk of premature foreclosure of identities. Focus group participants in research carried out by multiple intelligence author, Howard Gardner, and his colleague, Katie Davies, believed that the *App Generation* do form their identities with a higher external orientation than pre-digital youth (2013, p.66). My concern is that a highly sensitive external locus of evaluation that constantly looks outside for reassurance means that healthy identity formation could be severely inhibited. If this is true, it has significant implications for the identity formation of children within and without the Church as well as their spirituality, because their sense of belonging and connectedness in children and young people might be skewed.

Another concern of a number of writers is the impact digital media has on the increasingly transient nature of relationships. This disquiet is echoed in Turkle's *Alone Together* (2011), where she concludes that many people are already reliant on multi-media technology to provide relationships that, while lacking the complexities of human partnerships, could be considered to be 'emotionally dumbed down' (2011, p.6). This 'disposable love' phenomenon is not limited to adults and teenagers; arguably electronic pet toys allow children to have the fun associated with a pet without any of the reality and responsibility.

Gardner and Davies' research revealed the odd phenomenon that young people reveal the most intimate information online and then revert to perfunctory and distant interactions offline. This could be an indication of the lack of maturity that children and young people bring to online friendships as they develop competencies for creating and sustaining close and meaningful personal relationships. There is a distinction between having friends like the many we have on Facebook, and the few 'real' friends we may have. High-quality friendship is characterised by high levels of positive pro-social behaviours such as support and intimacy and low levels of negative features such as rivalry and conflict. It is peer acceptance that is believed to promote the development of those high-quality friendships and social competence, and peer rejection that inhibits them. The question is how this acceptance and rejection is mediated through digital technology for children, when we know that for teenagers much of their affirmation is based on criteria such as how many 'likes' a post has on Facebook and how many 'followers' they have on Twitter.

A Facebook friend is always available

One of the most significant negative impacts often associated with higher amounts of screen time is the reduction in the amount of time children are engaged in play, and in particular, free play, outdoor play and imaginative play. There is mounting evidence across multiple disciplines that links diminishing amounts of time to engage in various forms of play to negative outcomes for children including obesity, anxiety and depression, and decreased social competence (Marano 2008; Ogden *et al.* 2014). Research concerning what has been described as 'Generation C' – the 'connected generation' – suggests that children's overall media exposure has grown exponentially, with Ofcom statistics suggesting that 21 per cent of three- to four-year-olds have a tablet, a percentage that rises to 52 per cent for eight- to eleven-year-olds, 39 per cent of whom in addition have a smartphone. Using Ofcom statistics for eight- to eleven-year-olds, and making sweeping generalisations about the 'average child', it is easy to see how an 'average child's' day could be spent, and therefore how little time there is for free play:

- sleep – 10 hours (based on the minimum they need, not what many of them get!)

- meals – 1.5 hours

- school – 6 hours

- travel – 1 hour

- TV – 2 hours

- gaming – 1.5 hours

- online – 2 hours

- total – 24 hours.

Now I know that there is some overlap – for instance, it is difficult to identify the distinction between gaming and online activity, and many families eat their meals while watching television – but even without extra-curricular activities scheduled by parents, there is clearly very little space in the 'average child's' life to make some of the deeper emotional connections required for healthy spirituality and mental wellbeing.

A Facebook friend is not always available

Connected presence (Christensen 2009) is also becoming a feature of family life, where mobile phone use maintains intimate relationships and contact, and allows parents and carers to show affection to their families while managing a busy life. The downside is that this digital connection can replace rather than augment real connections and intimacy developed through face-to-face conversation, touch and personal encounter. Another effect of the mobile access is the 'over-connection' and surveillance related to what has been dubbed 'helicopter parenting', where parents available 24/7 over-protect their offspring right through to adulthood, and 'solve' all their problems for them, which means that children appear to be less resilient. Some believe that this, alongside a cultural emphasis on 'happiness', has been a contributing factor in the increased levels of depression and associated mental health issues in children and young people. Turkle (2011) uses the metaphor of a 'tether' when discussing the relationship between a young person and their digital device and the people they can access through it – the positive aspect being deep connection and security, the negative being control and captivity. One phenomenon being discussed is 'presence', with Watkins (2009) suggesting that for teenagers social media offers opportunities for 'presence-in-absence', that is, being with friends while not there, and 'absence-in-presence', being where you have to be but absenting yourself via technology.

Actions for helping children form healthy social connections

So there are positive and negative aspects for the connected generation, but what can we do, as fellow travellers in this digital age, to foster deep connections for children?

- Work with parents on supporting them to manage screen time effectively with their children and offer safe spaces for both the children and their parents to talk about their relationships and what they can do to improve them.

- Offer times of stillness, silence, rough-and-tumble play and appropriate touch. All these things, along with free play, can help children to self-regulate their emotions and negotiate development of social competence.

- Consider what policies your church and children's work need for online engagement and phone use in sessions.

- Make sure children know how to be safe, without destroying relationships with adults. Children, parents and carers may need reminding that not all adults are predators, and not all online connections are safe.

- Improve the transivity of children by increasing connections between different groups and in particular, different generations within the Church. This requires creating safe spaces for inter-generational contact and activity.

QUESTIONS FOR REFLECTION AND DISCUSSION

- How do you model effective relationships? When are you present but absent, or absent when present?

- What boundaries for online social media engagement and phone use during sessions should be discussed and agreed with children and their parents and carers?

- How can you communicate the importance of intergenerational connectivity to the wider Church?

References

boyd, d. (2014) *It's Complicated: The Social Lives of Networked Teens.* London and New York: Yale University Press.

Children's Society, The (2017) *The Good Childhood Report 2017.* Available at www.childrenssociety. org.uk/the-good-childhood-report-2017

Christakis, N. and Fowler, J. (2011) *Connected: The Amazing Power of Social Networks and How They Shape Our Lives.* London: HarperCollins.

Christensen, T.H. (2009) '"Connected presence" in distributed family life.' *New Media & Society 11*(3), 433–451.

Gardner, H. and Davies, K. (2013) *The App Generation: How Today's Youth Navigate Identity, Intimacy, and Imagination in a Digital World.* London and New York: Yale University Press.

Gross, E.F. (2005) 'Adolescent internet use: What we expect, what teens report.' *Applied Developmental Psychology 25*(6), 633–649.

Heim, J., Brandtzaeg, P.B., Hertzberg Kaare, B., Endestad, T. and Torgersen, L. (2007) 'Children's usage of media technologies and psychosocial factors.' *New Media & Society 9*(3), 425–454.

Marano, H. (2008) *A Nation of Wimps: The High Cost of Invasive Parenting.* New York: Broadway Publishing.

Moore, C. (2009) 'Fairness in children's resource allocation depends on the recipient.' *Psychological Science 20*, 944–948.

Ogden, C., Carroll, M.D., Kit, B.K. and Flegal, K.M. (2014) 'Prevalence of childhood and adult obesity in the United States, 2011–2012.' *Journal of American Medical Association 311*(8), 806–814.

Pea, R., Nass, C., Meheula, L., Rance, M. *et al.* (2012) 'Media use, face-to-face communication, media multitasking, and social well-being among 8- to 12-year-old girls.' *Developmental Psychology* *48*(2), 327–336.

Turkle, S. (2011) *Alone Together: We Expect More from Technology and Less from Each Other.* New York: Basic Books.

Watkins, S.C. (2009) *The Young & The Digital: What the Migration to Social Network Sites, Games, and Anytime, Anywhere Media Means for Our Future.* Boston, MA: Beacon Press.

Chapter 4

GRACIOUS GRANDPARENT

Working with Families

Martyn Payne

The future of society requires the fruitful encounter between young and old.

(Tweeted by Pope Francis, 15 June 2016)

Some social perspectives on the changing role of grandparents

Since becoming a grandparent myself, I've found that a lot has changed. Not long ago I was part of a day of storytelling in a school in Essex. Also on that day, a visiting Bishop from Kenya was with us. When I was introducing myself in the assembly, I said that I had recently become a grandpa, at which point the Bishop spoke up and asked the name of my new grandchild. Isaac, I told him. Then you should introduce yourself as 'Grandpa Isaac' – that's the way we do it in East Africa.

Just as becoming a parent for the first time is a huge transition point in life, so, too, is becoming a grandparent. You have a new name, a new relationship within the family, and new possibilities. And particularly in the Western world at the moment, grandparents are playing an increasingly important role. Grandparents are everywhere: on the school run, in the playground, reading to children in the classroom, pushing buggies in the park and playing football in the garden. And as providers of childcare, they have never been more indispensable to working parents. According to government statistics, nearly three out of five grandparents look after one or more children when the mother or father goes back to work (Working Families 2016). Grandparents are contributing in other ways, too, part-financing mortgages for their children and making sacrifices from savings to help out their family. And it seems likely that these percentages are set to increase with wealth continuing to be unequally distributed between the generations.

Many grandparents are involved in this new demanding world, even though they are often themselves still working and so, rather than enjoying the imagined idyll of leisurely retirement, they are instead juggling complicated schedules and travel in support of their children and grandchildren. Although it is still largely grandmothers who make up this care force, new research from the charity Grandparents Plus shows that grandfathers, too, are living longer, healthier lives, and that they are playing a bigger part in a family's support system.[1]

The role of grandparents and older people is being totally rewritten today. However, it is not just all about duty and hard work. Because grandparents are free from the ultimate responsibility of child rearing, they are able instead to enjoy activities and mischief that they never had time for when their own children were young. Some of the greatest gifts we can give to our grandchildren are those of time, free play and space to be. Walking along the road to school together, taking time to notice things, making cakes and a mess together in the kitchen, going on bus-top adventures or simply climbing a tree in the park, these are all precious moments of comfortable space that grandparents and grandchildren can gift each other, each vital to the grandchildren's health and wellbeing as much as to the grandparents'.

Increasingly grandparents are also a steadying influence in children's lives, particularly when the relationship between parents breaks down. In recent years there has been a growth in kinship carers, which is when grandparents have taken on the legal guardianship of their grandchildren through Child Arrangement Orders. The charity Grandparents Plus offers support, especially for those raising grandchildren full time, and campaigns for hands-on grandparents to have the right to flexible working hours and time off as their grandchildren grow up. This may be something new in the global North, but it has been happening informally for some time in the South, where the role of grandparents has been vital when parents have died of AIDS or have been forced to flee homes because of war or political instability.

However, parallel to these developments, the increased incidence of breakdown in marital relationships has sometimes sadly led to estrangement between grandchildren and grandparents. For these

---

1   See www.grandparentsplus.org.uk/grandparenting-in-europe-the-health-and-wellbeing-of-grandparents-caring-for-grandchildren

grandparents, there is the pain of never making that life-giving connection with their grandchildren, or only doing so under strained and uncomfortable circumstances. Likewise, those grandparents who have families who have moved away to other countries experience the pain of separation: despite the wonders of modern technology to help them connect on a screen, nothing can quite replace snuggling up close in each other's arms.

PAUSE FOR REFLECTION

- What was your experience of your own grandparents, and how might this be different today for your children and your children's children?

- We are always being told we have an ageing population in the Western world, but at the same time, because of better healthcare, those over retirement age are more likely to remain fit and active for longer. What might this mean for relationships between the generations in a family?

- Government statistics reveal that older people will form a majority of the British population by 2025. Within church congregations this is already the case, where the average age for attenders is 62 and rising. What role might grandparents and older people have in maintaining positive relationships between the generations within this sort of society?

Insights from research on the unchanged role of grandparents

In recent years there has been a growth of interest and research into the area of intergenerational relationships. This is partly driven by the changing demographic of Western societies, where the newly retired and older people make up an increasing percentage of our populations. In addition, highly individualised and mobile lifestyles have meant that some older people have become either isolated at home or separated in residential care away from families. Research into this area has highlighted the dangers of this separation and its repercussions. A healthy society needs intergenerational communities, where old and young can learn with and from each other. It should be noted at this point that churches have a unique role to offer in making this possible.

Grandparents are usually those who hold the bigger family story for their grandchildren, and where it is told faithfully, coming to know that family history can make an important contribution to a child's sense of self-worth and wellbeing. Interest in our family history, seen in programmes such as *Who Do You Think You Are?* or in stories of reconnecting parents, children and siblings such as in documentaries like *Long Lost Families* bear witness to this important element in all of our lives. Acquiring more knowledge about their family history can usually give children some sense of control over their own lives. In addition, knowing a family's 'big story narrative' can be linked to positive identity formation and increase their ability to show resilience when facing stress. Finding the metanarrative for our lives has never been more important than today, particularly when families face trauma or become irrevocably fractured. This is when a sense of belonging to something bigger and lasting can be a lifeline, and this is exactly what grandparents or older relatives can provide.

There is also a special bond between grandparents and grandchildren that makes this sort of conversation possible. They both represent those who live close to the edges of life, where neither generation is caught up in the messy business of living that occupies most of our middle years, where it seems all about making a name and finding security for ourselves through work. In this sense, old and young are on the margins or thresholds of life and death, and can form a special relationship, and often even conspiracy with each other. This generational connection is vital for the health of the whole of our society, where both the oldest and the youngest have time to listen to the other and hopefully together help balance the cares and concerns of those caught in the middle.

Recent research within the Church, too, has also highlighted these perspectives, noting that those who have remained rooted in the Church have done so because of the space and respect given to them by those of other generations around them. Similarly, it has been suggested that faith is much more likely to stick where it is caught and taught within an intergenerational congregation. In the Western world grandparents usually still come from a generation that at least remembers the stories of faith from their youth, often in contrast to their own children who have walked away from church, at least for the time being. Grandparents are often those who have a faith story to share, and so can have a significant role to play in the faith formation of the next generation. There may also be something in the suggestion that those who are near the beginning or near the end of their lives have a greater spiritual awareness of the presence of God. This can mean that they not only help each other into faith but, by extension, make it more possible for everyone to come closer to God as together they offer this gift of innate or rediscovered spirituality to all of us. In a post-Christian, Western world with many militant non-Christian or at least highly secular world views surrounding our grandchildren, the spiritual influence and impact of grandparents and older people with a living faith cannot be underestimated and, though a lone voice sometimes, is potentially more influential than they might realise.

In my experience, however, many Christian grandparents do nevertheless feel a sense of failure that for a variety of reasons their faith has not yet been caught by their own children. I note that they do not give up hope, but continue to pray for them and their children as well for other children with whom they work sacrificially within their churches, and for whom they are 'honorary grandparents'. We explore some of the practical ways forward for doing this later in the chapter.

PAUSE FOR REFLECTION

- Who holds the big story of your family's life? How is it told and shared across the generations?

- What positive experiences have you had of intergenerational connections?

- In what ways might grandchildren and grandparents share similar experiences and insights from the respective extremes of life's journey?

- From your own experience, how do we best share faith with our children and our children's children?

A biblical perspective on old and young together

When it comes to exploring what the Bible says about grandparents and grandchildren, we need to be cautious. The Old Testament is written within a particular cultural context where many of our modern issues of ageism, segregation and the nuclear family were unknown. And in the New Testament we hear mostly about a young church eagerly awaiting Christ's return, and so it seems that not much attention is given to issues of growing older. Nevertheless, there are examples of tensions around the tradition of the elders being at odds with new thinking – particularly, of course, in Jesus's life and words about those very traditions – but also of old and young learning with and from each other, all of which offer us principles from which to learn.

In the Hebrew tradition, faith was passed on through the extended family or tribe, who together enjoyed festivals, feasts and family meals together where the stories were told and acted out. Already there is a model here for us to rediscover. Rather than relying on dedicated teaching slots either for children in Sunday school or 'the all-age talk' or indeed on the sermon for adults, what is important is passed on in community and conversation at special events to commemorate the milestones of faith. As most grandparents will testify, it is faith conversations and God-talk that springs up naturally when we are doing something together with our grandchildren that really counts, far more than many a staged and often slightly cringe-worthy 'opening-the-Bible' moment.

Scripturally the role of older people – or to use a more recognisable Bible term, 'the patriarchs and matriarchs' – in the family was to pass on 'the story' and 'the blessing' in the home. It certainly wasn't franchised out to another place such as the synagogue, which, in fact, only became a feature of the Jewish tradition after the Babylonian exile. In the early stories of the Old Testament we read that the elders passed on the blessing of God to their children and grandchildren and indeed, whole chapters are devoted to these words of blessing. In a similar way Moses pronounced God's blessing on the tribes of Israel as 'a grandfather of the nation'. It is worth noting in this context that the word 'blessing' is a rich one and contains within it the sense of calling out the best of a person in response to God's love and grace. It isn't some mysterious charisma from on high landing on someone through prayer, but rather a prayer that each one of us will discover who we are meant to be as God's beloved children, and that we will go on to fulfil that in our living. Surely this is the sort of blessing grandparents want for their grandchildren and indeed, often the presence of grandchildren draws out the best of us as grandparents too!

Although the Old Testament largely reinforces the idea that wisdom is among those who are older, there are nevertheless some interesting stories that remind us that the wise should always be ready to learn from and listen to those who are younger. The young Elihu sits through the long speeches of Job's three older comforters before he offers his own 'wisdom of youth' (Job 32). Although what he says may not provide Job with the answers, he does have a flash of insight, recognising that in the end it is God's Spirit that imparts understanding to young and old alike (Job 32.8).

Even more strikingly, it is the young Samuel who brings insight to the elderly priest Eli (1 Samuel 1–3). Eli is like a spiritual grandfather or godparent to Samuel, training him in the ways of worship at Shiloh. Notably Eli's own children have betrayed the faith and, although priests themselves are using their position for their own benefit, it is the relationship between the older person and the young child in the story that is special and which in the end becomes a source of blessing for the whole of Israel. Yet it is to the boy Samuel that God chooses to speak with a message that is hard and one that Eli has been reluctant to hear. This story says so much about how spiritually aware young children already are, and how we can often learn things about God from them which in old age we have forgotten or never knew. Is it not often the case that the playful, wondering curiosity of a grandchild can reawaken in us as grandparents a new appreciation of the gift of life and God's amazing creation?

Perhaps the most telling image of intergenerational joy comes in the prophecy of Zechariah (8.1–8), where God gives him a vision of the new society that will come after the exile and which will be characterised by older and younger people happily present with each other. The old are not marginalised because they are not economically productive, nor the young ridiculed for their playfulness, but instead both are respected and find a shared space in the New Jerusalem. This togetherness is a challenge to many of our churches that have, on the whole, thought it best to separate ages when it comes to gathered worship. And yet we miss so much if we are silo-ed off like this, and it certainly isn't what is prophesied here. How can I, as an older person, continue to be open to new things without the stimulation of the presence of a child whose curiosity is endless? And how can a child discover what has been experienced to be a safe and good way to live without the guidance of an older person? What is true for everyday living is even more so when it comes to exploring the infinite dimensions of faith in God.

An important story from the New Testament that offers us some insights into grandparenting comes early in Luke's Gospel. Joseph and Mary take the baby Jesus to the Temple and there they encounter Simeon and Anna. Although not specifically mentioned as old, Simeon seems to represent those of a grandparent age, and certainly Anna who joins him there is, we are told, of an age that she could have been a great grandmother. Neither is related to Jesus by blood, but both rejoice to see the young child as God's Messiah for whom they have long waited. Simeon prays a blessing over Jesus and a prophecy over Mary, while Anna can't contain her joy and becomes an evangelist among the Temple worshipers, no doubt telling them that the light of the world has come.

For me this story in the Temple highlights something special about the new family of God into which we can all come, whether we have children of our own or not, or indeed might never become grandparents. The child, the mother, the stepfather, Simeon and great grandma Anna are old and young together related by grace, and give us a New Testament glimpse of Zechariah's Old Testament prophecy where the generations find peace with one another in the New Jerusalem, or as we might term it, the Kingdom of God. As part of my work for the Bible Reading Fellowship (BRF), I have visited a lot of churches, particularly the new shape of church called 'Messy Church', and there I often become a *gracious grandparent* to children not of my own family, but God's. Whether grandparents or not, when we reach a certain age it is possible that God has a new grandparent-like ministry for us with the children of our church or in our community. God offers us new possibilities of service, and this also reminds me of a prayer we find in the Psalms, where the writer prays 'Even when I'm old and grey, do not forsake me, my God, until I declare your power to the next generation, your mighty acts to all who are to come' (Psalm 71.18). This might have been Lois's prayer for example, who is described as a woman of faith (2 Timothy 1.5), and who helped pass on that faith as grandmother to her grandson Timothy. It can be our prayer too.

Finally, there is one prophecy that comes from the Old Testament in the book of Joel, but which becomes key to an understanding of the gift of the Holy Spirit when the Church is born on the day of Pentecost. Joel prophesied that the Spirit would come like this, on old and young alike, gifting them with dreams and visions respectively (Joel 2.28–29 and Acts 2.17ff). This prophecy of a harmony between the generations was always part of God's plan but one that the Church and society have struggled to realise. It's easier to put people into boxes and keep the generations separate, treating their concerns and needs in isolation, whereas the truth is that God has created us to need each other, both young and old. We need each other's dreams and visions in order to become whole people. This is also Paul's 'body of Christ' metaphor for the Church from his letters and which we see worked out in practice in the mixed age, gender and social groupings that made up the first Christian communities across the Mediterranean. Jesus came to break down barriers, not to build them, and perhaps grandparents and older members of congregations can do something about this in our day, reaching out across the generations to children and the children's children to restore a harmony in family relationships and to offer foundations for faith nurture.

> **PAUSE FOR REFLECTION**
>
> • How might faith be shared within families today through meals and special celebrations in a positive and lasting way?
>
> • In what ways can grandparents and grandchildren be a blessing to each other?
>
> • The Psalmist prays 'Teach me to number my days that I might get a heart of wisdom' (Psalm 90.12). What is the 'wisdom of the young' or 'the wisdom of the old', and how do we learn it? (See also James 3.17.)
>
> • How can churches facilitate gathered worship that allows young and old to grow in faith together?

Some practical ways forward for working with families

As we have noted already, patterns of family life in our Western society are changing, including if and when people decide to get married and also when they have children, if at all. Among some social groupings where both partners have fulfilling careers for which they have trained, it is not uncommon for them to wait until later to have children. Understandably, they then also both wish to carry on with their work, and this often brings in the 'grandparent factor'. Many people of retirement age and older find themselves busier than ever. However, one positive side effect of this is bringing the generations together. Even in some communities that are less affluent, the same thing happens, but this time it is driven by the need to support each other when money is tight and affordable housing is difficult to find. In both cases the generations are reconnecting, whether because of financial pressures or life choices. Churches need to recognise this and offer opportunities where old and young in this way can integrate and discover how to be together in a creative way.

There are many ways in which the Church can encourage old and young to be together both within and beyond gathered services. Some fresh expressions such as 'Messy Church' have made being all-age one of their foundational values, seeking to create a safe place where old and young can learn and worship together. Others have re-imagined what used to be called 'all-age' or 'family worship', recognising that everyone of whatever age might have different preferred learning and spiritual styles, and this means that old and young should be welcomed at all the activities provided. However, despite the best attempts to integrate the generations, the fact is that, unless it is modelled within the home, then lasting faith cannot be passed on and nurtured adequately. This is where older people, godparents and grandparents can come into their own.

Finding space and time for your grandchildren, when you can simply both 'be' without an agenda, is one of the best gifts any older person can offer a child. Joining in with their favourite activities, teaching inherited skills or learning new ones from the children of the digital age allow this to happen. Introducing children to family traditions from when you were a child, going through the old photo albums and being honest about our own failures through life in a way that may be difficult for parents and letting them know how having faith has made a difference, this can fuel those moments and turn them into precious times with each other and with God. And even for those who live far away, new communication possibilities via the internet mean that you can still be together even in a virtual way as often as possible. Even so, don't forget the power of letters as well, which have now become a rarity in our culture. There's still nothing like opening an envelope and seeing someone's own handwriting which tells you that someone has taken the time to communicate with you personally!

Many grandparents and grandchildren carry fond memories of special holidays together. We should never underestimate the power of these occasions for building relationships and faith. Camping, long walks, even going on a humanitarian mission trip together can become significant rites of passage for children at a particular age, and will offer countless opportunities for shared conversations that can go very deep. In a similar way, a shared project can also be life-giving, as you bake cakes for a charity sale, organise and complete a sponsored walk, or get involved in the local food bank – young and old together. There are already several secular organisations and initiatives that are encouraging this sort of intergenerational partnership, particularly in schools where older people are invited to come in and share memories with children, and also children, accompanied by teachers, visit local care homes. Churches should be encouraging this too, looking for creative ways in which they can offer opportunities for young or old to serve together as part of their mutual discipleship.

Being gracious grandparents is far more than choosing an appropriate children's Bible to give to your grandchild as a birthday gift or vainly dropping hints about taking them to church rather than to the football match. In fact, it's probably much more about going to that football match and being supportive, and about finding ways in which you can share each other's interests. A conversation about God in this context can be worth more than many church visits or Sunday school sessions. Rather than feeling guilty as too many grandparents and older people do about the spiritual state of their children and grandchildren, we should take a more positive approach which includes, of course, praying, but also learning how to walk alongside each other as people with faith, and building an ever-deepening friendship which is then much more likely to bear fruit for eternity.

> Praise the Lord!... Young men and women alike, old and young together... Let them praise the name of the Lord. (Psalm 148)

QUESTIONS FOR REFLECTION AND DISCUSSION

- How can we, as churches, affirm the role of grandparents, godparents and other older people as a spiritual calling that offers a role model for those who are younger?

- What are the best gifts you can give to a child either in your family or within the family of the Church? And what gifts can children and young people give to you?

- If you were asked to give a talk in church about creative ways for bringing faith into everyday life at home and between the generations, what would you highlight?

- 'Become friends with people who aren't your age; hang out with people whose first language isn't the same as yours; get to know someone who doesn't come from your social class; this is how you see the world. This is how you grow' (Anon.). Reflect on this quote and how it might apply to relationships between old and young, grandparents and grandchildren, in your context.

Online resources

Fuller Institute and Sticky Faith have done some interesting research on the role of grandparents in the lives of their grandchildren, both young ones and teenagers. Fuller Youth Institute (2013) 'Twenty ideas for grandparents.' Available at http://fulleryouthinstitute.org/articles/twenty-ideas-for-grandparents

Grandparents plus www.grandparentsplus.org.uk

Uniting Young People Australia, Great Grandparenting Seminar https://aifs.gov.au/cfca/publications/changing-rolegrandparents

References and further reading

Bengtson, V.L. (2017) *Families and Faith: How Religion is Passed Down across Generations.* Oxford: Oxford University Press.

Butcher, J. (2014) 'Ideas for exploring faith in homes.' Bible Reading Fellowship, 28 April. Available at www.faithinhomes.org.uk/ideas-for-grandparents-and-older-people-to-support-children

Collicutt, J. (2014) *Reflections on the Bible and Old Age, October 2014 Guidelines.* Abingdon: Bible Reading Fellowship.

Graham, B. (2011) *Nearing Home: Life Faith and Finishing Well.* Nashville, TN: Thomas Nelson.

Grice, E. (2016) 'The age of the "grands": The pleasures and pitfalls of modern grandparenting.' *Weekend Telegraph*, 27 August. Available at www.telegraph.co.uk/women/family/the-age-of-the-grands-the-pleasures-and-pitfalls-of-modern-grand

Hilborn, D. (2016) 'Respecting the old and favouring the young.' IDEA, 27 June. Available at www.eauk.org/idea/respecting-the-old-and-favouring-the-young.cfm

Payne, M. (2016) *Messy Togetherness.* Abingdon: Bible Reading Fellowship.

Winter, D. (2015) *At the End of the Day: Enjoying Life in the Departure Lounge.* Abingdon: Bible Reading Fellowship.

Working Families (2016) *Modern Families Index 2016.* Available at www.workingfamilies.org.uk/wp-content/uploads/2016/02/Modern-Families-Index-2016.pdf

Chapter 5

CLOWN AND FOOL

Fun and Play

Sian Hancock

Knock, knock.
Who's there?
Jester.
Jester who?
Jester minute – I'm still thinking!

Introduction

'Playing the clown' or 'acting the fool' are phrases that echo from my childhood. It wasn't so much a compliment, but more an accusation! Playing or acting could be interpreted as mimicking. The clown and fool are seen to be behaving comically or foolishly for the entertainment of others and not to be taken seriously. Often the reason for this behaviour was to detract from a sense of inferiority in the classroom or the bravado deflecting social exclusion. So what kind of metaphor is this for those in children's ministry?

To understand its relevance and to highlight something of its value and effect we need to consider the different models of clowns and fools. Following closely is laughter and how it is used in different ways for a range of effects. Travelling just a little further down this road leads us into exploring playfulness and its relationship with spirituality, so that we can recognise and respond to the need for more opportunities for fun, laughter and play in children's ministry – all of this as a reflection on the playful nature of the God in whose name we gather.

The court jester in medieval times was part of the royal household, a performer to entertain and bring laughter to the monarch and guests. They would also be called for to bring a smile when the monarch was unwell or angry. Some jesters travelled around the villages and towns performing as they went. The cloth hat of a jester was called a fool's hat, with each of its three points adorned with bells that would tinkle whenever the head moved. Dressed in a gaudy and humorous two-piece, the jester was believed to be delivering a message through his songs, riddles and rhymes.

My earliest experience of a clown was at Billy Smart's Circus. Brightly clothed with outsized shoes that he kept tripping over, the painted white-faced, red-nosed entertainer wore a frizzy orange wig topped with a lime-green bowler adorned with a flower that squirted water at his fellow clown. He made us laugh with his silly walk and inability to get things right. But he rarely said a word. His actions and facial expressions left the audience in no doubt about his feelings. That clown didn't scare me, his slapstick routine made me laugh, but years later, watching dramas on TV, I noticed the clown could be more sinister and scary, with less laughter and more menace. The ambiguity of play takes many guises, according to Sutton-Smith (1997): the circus clown and his slapstick humour raises the question is this serious or nonsense, the ambiguity of sense. It might also question the clown's intent – does he mean to to be clumsy or is he pretending? Similarly there is ambiguity surrounding the clown on television. Perhaps similar in appearance but clearly emulating a different meaning – does this clown want to play or fight? Sutton-Smith argues that there are different perspectives on play – not dissimilar to laughter and humour – depending on our relationship with it.

In classical theatre there is often a fool whose voice speaks truth into difficult situations challenging the status quo, sometimes lightening the atmosphere while at other times offering a satirical narrative on recent events. Although dressed comically, Shakespeare's fool was often the misfit, on the edge of society, speaking prophetic insights to those seeking wisdom.

Laughter can take several forms, from mockery to satirical subversion, with irony and sarcasm mixed in. John Morreall's (1983) study of laughter set out four models: first, *superiority*, where one is laughing at another person. Second, the *incongruity* model that focuses on thinking rather than feeling. Third, the *relief* model that gives vent to nervous or surplus energy. Finally, the *pleasant psychological shift* model (Morreall's own) that recognises laughter as the physical activity caused by a shift in feeling, including both sensory and perceptual shifts such as surprise – 'Serious laughter signals that one is experiencing a playful, meditative, and creative sense of life, rather than the sneer of controlling rigidity and the endless hilarity of madness' (Berryman 1998, p.368). Our capacity for humour becomes more sophisticated as we mature intellectually and emotionally.

If, as Berryman argues, serious laughter is what arises with delight from the complexity of life, then as Christians of all ages we should be guided by the sound of laughter to draw nearer to God.

Perspectives on fun, humour and playing the clown

Distinguishing between the laughter of delight, as we read of Sarah's response, incongruous at first, to the prophetic vision of having a son (Genesis 18), and later in delight at the birth of Isaac (Genesis 21), and the laughter of scorn like that of the Old Testament Psalmist, is a challenge, especially within a group of children. There can be a fine line between the two, and yet a wave of emotion that distinguishes the two. Laughter can signal the haughty scorn of the victor in a repressive power struggle or the winning team in a game. Other laughter can express the delight of discovering something for yourself and perhaps relief at working it out, like the child who discovers a new fresh insight to a Bible story. Children's workers need to become connoisseurs of laughter to guide their teaching (Berryman 1998, p.358). Perhaps alongside this, an understanding of play is helpful as it can be the catalyst for laughter.

When we think about church and ministry, play doesn't readily come to mind. However, there are a lot of different types of play to be seen in the work we do with children; they just may not be spoken of in the language of play.

What is play?

Play can be fun and enjoyable, but it can also be deep and emotionally hard, especially in a therapeutic context. So at times it may bring relaxation and refreshment – a renewing of energy; at other times it may inspire and motivate inquiry to find meaning; and sometimes it can bring restoration and healing. Jenkinson (2001) endorses the restorative nature of play writing: 'Children's wellbeing is enhanced by their play: their bodies are exercised, their imaginations stimulated, their cognitive skills developed, and they can rest afterwards' (2001, p.137).

The motive to play is intrinsic. We are biologically wired to play. The qualities and benefits of play enrich us psychologically, physically, socially, educationally and spiritually. Our lives do indeed need a balance of work, rest and play!

Play is spontaneous and freely chosen. It is the player who determines and controls the content and intent of their play by following their instincts, ideas and interests, in their own way for their own reasons.

Children's play can sometimes mask its own complexity. What may appear to only be a game will often be children 'playing a game of their own invention and making and breaking the rules as they go along. While playing these self-initiated games is fun, it also helps children learn the interpersonal skills needed to become effective social beings' (Elkind 2007, p.145).

Play involves active engagement. The autonomy of play liberates the player to immerse themselves. Deep play is understood to be where the player becomes so pre-occupied with what they are doing that they are oblivious to events and people around them, emotionally and cognitively. To discover this for oneself rather than following the instructions or directions of another makes this transcendence more tangible.

Play works non-literally. Play is phenomenal; it comes from a sense perception, which means that even the same play experience can have a different impact on two individuals. It can seem an elusive mystery, ambiguous in nature, not dissimilar to the parabolic teachings of Jesus with the invitation to play with meaning.

What is happening when children play?

There is a cyclical process occurring when children play called the 'play cycle'. It begins with an individual's impulse (or 'drive') to play that sends out a 'cue' to another person or the environment to join in; this might be the catching of the eye of another or calling out a name or even throwing an object at a wall. The 'play return' is the response from the other person or the environment, that is, the ball bounces back off the wall or the person runs across in response to their name. The 'play frame' is the boundary or environment surrounding this play/interaction (Brown and Taylor 2008). The fragility of this play frame needs to be protected so when an adult is facilitating play they are watchful and attentive to its evolution, ready to intervene if necessary, but also aware that inappropriate intervention can disturb and break its flow. This may seem to subvert the usual order of adults, leading children to being the adult led by the child/ren. Perhaps it could be argued that it is a biblical vision of the Kingdom of God (Isaiah 11.6).

A simplified biblical example of the play cycle can be seen in the story of Jonah. The cue is God calling Jonah to go to Nineveh. There is no return as Jonah runs away on the ship to Tarshish. So God sends another cue in the form of a storm. This time the return occurs when the sailors throw Jonah overboard, where he is swallowed by a large fish. The large fish spews up Jonah onto the shore, a cue for Jonah to join in.

Jonah decides to sit out under the tree (his return). The game continues until finally Jonah fulfils what God is asking of him. Who is playing with whom in this story? Applying the play cycle to Scripture in this way may help to illustrate something of the playful nature of God while beginning to build a connection between play (the ordinary everyday activity of children) and spirituality (the awareness of some greater 'other') as a footstep to faith.

What types of play do we see in children's ministry?

The play seen in children's ministry will be determined by the age and stage of the children as well as the context in which they are meeting. The toddler group allows for locomotor play through movement, including, but not exclusively, the use of ride-on toys and indoor climbing frames/slides. The Sunday School may focus more on dramatic play that explores ways of being by re-enacting the biblical story and children putting themselves into the story. Older groups may use more communication play to discuss, argue and reason, as they theologically reflect or use words to create prayers, poems and raps to express their worship. All-age worship helps recapitulative play as traditions and rituals in church are experienced and understood. Creative play features in most contexts but is a key feature of 'Messy Church' as biblical concepts and stories are explored through crafts, and a response can be made using a range of materials. Object and symbolic play, using infinite and interesting sequences of hand-eye manipulations and movements, can be experienced through Godly Play, for example.

What does it mean to clown, fool or 'be an idiot for Christ'?

We are fools for the sake of Christ, but you are wise in Christ

(1 Corinthians 4.10)

In his book, *Images of Pastoral Care*, Robert Dykstra (2005) highlights the paradox of being a wise fool, and explores this and the image of the clown in ministry. It is a challenging paradox, but what does it mean for us in children's work? It's easy to think it means always clowning around, like a holiday camp entertainer whose performance engages, bringing laughter from the children present as one trick, action song or joke leads to another. As much as children enjoy having fun, there are times when children want to be more reflective and are pensive, preferring quiet and deeper thinking. Sometimes the counter-cultural slower pace and times of silence is the gift the Church can give to children in the busyness of their week in today's fast-moving society.

Being an advocate for children in the local church can be like the voice of the prophet speaking from the margins. Those listening may not be ready to *hear and act* on those words, and may not understand the underlying challenge. How do we determine wise words from nonsense? Some may see it as foolhardy, but if you are passionate about nurturing children's spirituality, there will be a commitment to this that may, at times, cause you to challenge your local church community and alienate you in your role (Matthew 18.3). It may require a sense of setting aside yourself to bring about change for the children in your care (Matthew 16.25). Sometimes being the fool is necessary and significant (1 Corinthians 1.21).

Being the fool can sometimes mean being the scapegoat – which is not a comfortable position to be in. When the numbers of children attending church is not changing, eyes may look to the children's worker as if they are the only one responsible for growing the church, yet it is the mission of the Church and all Christians to go and tell (Matthew 28.19).

Love often causes us to be foolish (1 Corinthians 1.25). The art of caring without considering what personal cost it may have is not something the world understands but something it questions – why would you do that? It is part of God's upside-down Kingdom that makes no sense as it subverts the norms of society and highlights juxtapositions like the wise fool. It may also be here where there can be a sense of having the last laugh as the fool – it makes no sense, yet it brings about the required response. Let me explain what I mean. There is a perception among adults of knowing what children enjoy, want and need. This is often informed by the latest trends, consumerist values and mimicking what is seen to be successful in contemporary culture. So when a different approach is taken that seemingly goes against the stream of popular opinion, it gives children a tangible sense of belonging in their own right, an opportunity and safe space to search, question and wrestle for meaning and understanding, the voice to articulate their prayers and the encouragement to be disciples of Jesus, the transformation isn't limited to the individual but ripples out to impact the worshipping community as a whole. This may seem risky – investing in the least – but the fool is no stranger to risk. The *fool* has already taken the risk of committing to the minority and those without voice in the power structures, to advocating on behalf of the marginalised who often go unseen away in the back rooms of the building or at times of the week when the majority of adults aren't about, to challenging the status quo of how things are done to advance the way and to change adult mindsets towards children, and to *poke fun* at some of the ways of being including themselves, to break down barriers and hierarchy and in doing so, raise the profile of children, their spirituality and their discipleship.

The drama of playing or unmasking the fool?

According to Faber (1971), the circus clown lives with three key tensions:

- of belonging to a team (the circus) and being in isolation (a solo act)

- of appearing to be and feeling like an amateur among acknowledged experts (others performing skilful stunts while the clown's foolishness achieves little more than laughter)

- of the need to be original and creative amidst the routine and familiarity.

These tensions could also be applied to those in children's ministry. First, not all children's workers are invited to the top table (seen to be part of the leadership/ministry team). Some in paid roles are managing a team of volunteers, but as the employed worker they are ultimately responsible for shaping and leading the children's work. Second, while you are never *just* a children's worker, those working with children will often say this feeling inferior to others. I believe children's work is a huge privilege that keeps you grounded; it requires a distinct skill set to accompany children on their spiritual journey, but I know that it is not always held with the same regard as those who work with young people or adults. There are those within the Christian church who see children as *disciples in waiting* rather than as *young disciples already in a relationship with Jesus*. Practice and experience develops and refines the artistry of a children's worker to be attentive to the nurture of the God spark within a child. Third, in a culture that is fast-moving, entertaining and optional, it is tempting to feel a need to keep reinventing the wheel as opposed to counter-culturally remaining distinctive and intentional about purpose and role.

Clowning is not so much a character to assume but an approach to thinking that is open-minded, curious and playful. It is a laying down of self and conformity to create opportunities to explore – where everything is possible and nothing is quite as it seems. There are a number of factors that capture attention and can evoke laughter. Alongside these I offer examples from children's work and a question for you to reflect on in relation to your own context:

- The incompetence of the physicality of the clown, their misdemeanours and the chaos that their actions bring empower the child. This can dispel the dynamic of the more experienced adult and the naivety of the child to drawing on the expertise of the child to show the adult how it's done. Technology is often a key example of this – the way children work with computers is often less inhibited than it is for the adults around them, and their intuitive approach to learning helps them achieve shortcuts and best results in ways adults may take a lot longer to discover. *When have you learned something from a child, how did it feel for you, and how did it affect the child?*

- Timing is crucial. Children are very much in the present – now is the time they are in church, now is the time for meaningful opportunities of belonging, discipleship and service. *Where are these opportunities for the children in your group to participate more fully in your worshipping community?*

- The rhythm and flow of their actions, coupled with both of the above, show a synchronicity and interconnection that together have impact. Rituals are important as they give meaning to significant times and ways of being. Having a clear flow or rhythm to your sessions helps the group to participate without worrying about what's going to happen next. It can be comforting and reassuring to know. *What is the framework that supports your children's work?*

- The element of surprise following a sense of anticipation adds dramatic effect but it also overcomes predictability that can be mundane. Sometimes the element of surprise is experienced as awe and wonder – the times when we may gasp in delight saying 'ahh', or perhaps it causes an 'ooo' with the shock of injustice. *How are spiritual 'aha' moments experienced in your setting?*

- Truth speaking through all the above is refreshing, enlightening and influential. Children's work is often done *for*, or done *to*, the group, whereas when it is done *with* the children, their ideas, reflections and insights can be enriching and inform future plans. Furthermore, when adults speak on behalf of children in the adult structures, they are able to speak with more conviction of what the children are thinking as their opinions have been voiced and heard. *Who is seeking out and listening for the voice of the children in your group?*

The key to clowning is having presence that holds attention and enables a good connection between the clown and their audience. It reminds me of public speaking and my own initial teacher training, in which the use of voice (tone and volume) as well as posture and effective non-verbal communication holds attention and enables clarity and coherency when speaking at the front in a classroom, school assembly hall or church lectern/pulpit. In children's ministry presence can also mean consistent commitment to accompanying children on their spiritual journey. In an age of rotas this is a challenge, but it is also even more vital to be that significant other. Connection (or we might say relationship) more naturally flows out of spending time, learning and sharing life together. It tells children they matter.

Truth speaking in children's ministry

When my daughters were young, we had a book of Aesop's Fables that they used to love reading. They enjoyed the short tales that often seemed absurd and subverted expectations, especially through talking animals! We used to take time to peel back the layers of the underlying meaning of the stories or moral message that was integral to it. In many ways, the creative storytelling playing with the natural order of human and animal behaviour to communicate a clear message is similar to the work of the court jester, and to the same end.

Often the gifts children share in our churches are applauded as if they are a performance rather than offered with the same spirit of service or worship as an adult might. It may be that the applause is an expression of thanks or an attempt to encourage, but I wonder how often it is expected that the child is moved by their own participation.

Truth speaking in children's ministry is as much about the work done with the children as it is about the work done with the adults. We are reminded that the court jesters or fools often said things others couldn't but in doing so created a 'protected context' for this purpose, 'the truth can be spoken in jest when it is implicitly understood that the intent is not to wound' (Bateson and Martin 2013, p.107). Helping others to understand the spirituality of childhood and the faith of children is key. When growing the work with children the work with adults will need to be prepared to understand that this is more than the numbers attending the groups or the potential and needs of future youth work. It will have been a long time for many since childhood, so remembering what it means to be a child and characteristics of children, as well as considering the implications of this as a child of God, means we can begin to reflect on what Jesus was talking about when he put the child in the centre.

There is an art to jesting and clowning that is easily mistaken with being entertaining, and the art of truth speaking can seem opaque and be lost on the listener. The most skilful are those who are able to poke fun at the powerholders yet remain in relationship. They remain working within the structures yet somehow turn the processes upside down to bring about change. They speak truth not to offend but to challenge thinking and confront nonsensical ways of being. They play with words to broaden meaning and show another way. So in good play work practice we might consider that the jester is motivated to play, and that drive helps them to send out a cue to perhaps those with influence. An example of this may be sending the child to the minister with their question. If there is a return to the cue, the cycle has begun, and the jester may continue to interact, so that there is an exchange or dialogue that playfully reimagines the way things may be. A word of warning comes in the tale of 'The Ass and the Lapdog', where the ass tries to imitate the dog climbing on to the farmer's lap to receive a treat as the dog had done – 'clumsy jesting is no joke!'

QUESTIONS FOR REFLECTION AND DISCUSSION

- Who might be the jesters in your setting?

- What aspects of clowning are you drawn to and why?

- Consider what play is already present within your work with children.

- Where could you include more playfulness in worship?

- How could play revolutionise the life of your church?

References and further reading

Bateson, P. and Martin, P. (2013) *Play, Playfulness, Creativity and Innovation.* Cambridge: Cambridge University Press.

Berryman, J.W. (1998) 'Laughter, power and motivation in Religious Education.' *Religious Education* 93(3), 358–377

Berryman, J.W. (2005) 'Playful orthodoxy: Reconnecting religion and creativity by education.' *Sewanee Theological Review* 48(4), 437–454.

Berryman, J. (2017) *Becoming Like a Child.* New York: Church Publishing Inc.

Brown, S. with Vaughan, C. (2010) *Play: How It Shapes the Brain, Opens the Imagination, and Invigorates the Soul.* London: Penguin.

Brown, F. and Taylor, C. (eds) (2008) *Foundations of Playwork.* Maidenhead: Open University Press.

Dykstra, R.C. (2005) *Images of Pastoral Care: Classic Readings*. Atlanta, GA: Chalice Press.

Elkind, D. (2007) *The Power of Play*. Philadelphia, PA: da Capo Books.

Faber, H. (1971) *Pastoral Care in a Modern Hospital*. London: Student Christian Movement.

Jenkinson, S. (2001) *The Genius of Play*. Stroud: Hawthorn Press.

Mainstone-Cotton, S. (2017) *Promoting Young Children's Emotional Health and Wellbeing*. London: Jessica Kingsley Publishers.

Morreall, J. (1983) *Taking Laughter Seriously*. New York: State University of New York Press.

Sutton-Smith, B. (1997) *The Ambiguity of Play*. London: Harvard University Press.

Chapter 6

CONSOLE CHAMPION

Playing with Technology

Andy Robertson

Introduction

Children grow up with screens and video games all around them. Whether or not they play a lot, it's familiar territory to young people. They understand how much fun it can be to immerse themselves in a virtual world, collaborate with others to build monstrous cathedrals, compete in imaginary new sports with people from all over the world, or just hear old stories told in new interactive ways. They know this isn't a passing fad, that it's not just something for children. They know it's the future, digital, global reality.

Parents also grew up with screens and video games in the world, but they were optional rather than ubiquitous. This means that while it may not be acceptable for adults to declare themselves non-readers who never intend to pick up a book, it is currently accepted to say you don't and never intend to play a video game. This divide makes it hard for parents, carers and children's workers to offer advice about screens and games, like they do in other areas. Children themselves don't mind, and happily stumble from one popular game to the next. However, without the usual guiding, reassuring and ambitious presence of adults, they are less likely to have the confidence, stability and understanding to make healthy choices, or to get the most from the games they play.

Young people and children understand the technology, but they are easily coerced towards mundane, monotonous or violent games by adverts and big game promotions. They know how to play games, but can be unaware of what games are doing to them. Children are drawn to the fun and entertainment of interactive battles, but don't realise there is a broader diet of games they might prefer.

As Shapiro (2018) argues, children readily develop the confidence to operate and experiment with digital tools, but it takes grown-ups to guide this development away from profiteering companies or repetitive entertainment and towards meaning and learning. This is the largely uncapitalised opportunity of video games. Rather than use them as a way to encourage attendance or to entertain, youth and children's work can shape how video games are seen and experienced in the lives of its young (and not so young) players.

I'm not suggesting that we turn each game into an allegory about faith, or a sermon opportunity. Rather, we can equip young people and children to interpret and expect more from the games they play. Along with the educational benefits games also offer new ways to encounter meaning and form an important part of children's spiritual identity. This may sound grandiose, particularly when so many games focus on shooting people in the head. However, faith communities are deeply experienced at dealing with complex violent texts, and not letting the killing eclipse their value. They also have literary interpretive tools that, although traditionally reserved for literature and Scripture, are perfectly placed to shed fresh light on video games.

We have some catching up to do. It requires us to develop not only a deep understanding of what video games are, but also a genuine relationship with their spiritual benefits. We need to have encountered their disarming, unsettling, joyous, fragile worlds and made sense of what they mean. This isn't easy to achieve. To guide someone's reading or viewing we must have read and watched ourselves. For adults to guide children to video game health and wellbeing, they need to become players too.

Dr Alastair Jones, who was CEO of Frontier Youth Trust for over five years, discovered the truth of this himself. He hadn't played many games but discovered that they could be a valuable part of both his personal and professional life. As he puts it:

> I found myself as an unlikely gamer, I would sometimes play FIFA with young people or Angry Birds, but it wasn't until playing through an entire game, Limbo, that I actually felt I had achieved something in the gaming world. But not only that – it moved me emotionally and personally affected the way I viewed the gaming world.

This led to him using video games regularly and successfully in his work with children and young people. It was a process that took some time and guidance. In the rest of this chapter I'll be laying out how this can be achieved, even by someone who, like Alastair, has rarely played modern games (and adamantly never expects to).

The dangers of video games

To understand video games better we need to be upfront about their dangers. This is an area where most academic papers or research end by saying 'more work needed'. We are only scratching the surface, but still, there are some very useful points being uncovered.

Screen time

This is a hot topic, with a lot of worry spent on how long is too long. However, a recent study from the Oxford Internet Institute and Cardiff University of 20,000 parents challenges simplistic time limits. It states that:

> …there is little or no support for the theory that digital screen use, on its own, is bad for young children's psychological wellbeing. If anything, our findings suggest the broader family context, how parents set rules about digital screen time, and if they're actively engaged in exploring the digital world together, are more important than the raw screen time. (Pryzbylski and Weinstein 2017)

Like a balanced diet, we need to think more about what's on the gaming plate than just time at the table. Developing ways for groups and families to treat playtime like mealtimes is a powerful take-home from this research, and something this chapter will help you do. We are used to the effort required to learn to cook, plan a menu, create healthy eating habits and create shared spaces in which to eat. We are less familiar, or willing to tackle, the work adults need to do to create a healthy and varied consumption of video games.

Addiction

Addiction is another concern for parents and children's workers. Research in 2017 by the University of Michigan Center for Human Growth and Development measured media addiction in four- to eleven-year-olds. They found that, 'how children use the devices, not how much time they spend on them, is the strongest predictor of emotional or social problems connected with screen addiction' (Domoff *et al.* 2017). Understanding how the children in our care are using technology, what is happening on the screen and how this makes them feel, is more important than how long they are wedded to their screens. To ensure health we need to have a deeper knowledge of how games work rather than police them as outsiders.

The Michigan study goes on to say that, 'What matters most is whether screen use causes problems in other areas of life or has become an all-consuming activity.' Understanding this will enable us to identify when games edge children towards the addictive behaviour described by the World Health Organization's (WHO) definition of 'gaming disorder',[1] and how to helpfully untangle the cause and effect of real issues.

Violence

Violent behaviour is another concern, particularly when younger children play games with an older age rating. There are worries that shooting in video games can lead to tragic real-world shootings. Although it might be easy to believe headlines that often suggest otherwise, evidence directly linking violent behaviour to the games children play is still inconclusive. For instance, results from research carried out in Singapore in 2014 suggest that video games that portray violence as fun, justified or without negative consequences have the potential to change a child's views on empathy and aggression (Gentile *et al.* 2014). Ferguson (2015), a psychologist at Stetson University in Florida, US, conducted a similar study in Florida in the same year, and concluded that playing video games is associated with less youth violence, and that increased societal violence cannot be predicted from levels of consumption of media violence.

Either way, what we need to be helping children with is deciphering the real from the virtual. The UK government's *Safer Children in a Digital World* (Byron 2008) review report highlighted age appropriateness as a key factor here, with younger children having a significantly limited ability to interpret content and distinguish what is real from fantasy.

Wellbeing

While screen time, addictive behaviour and video game violence may trigger concerns, there is increasing research showing how games have a positive impact and offer unique opportunities in this area. Video games can form part of a child's development of resilience as they create contexts where children can find belonging and safety, cope with stress, process their day, find support from friends and nurture confidence and self-esteem (Johnson *et al.* 2013). Capitalising on these benefits and avoiding detrimental effects on wellbeing requires children's workers, parents and carers to play a key role in creating healthy contexts for play. We need to

---

1   See www.who.int/features/qa/gaming-disorder/en

be able to aid interpretation and processing of these experiences to guide children towards wellbeing opportunities.

What video games are

This research underlines important work for those alongside children to steer video games towards being a healthy part of their lives. To do this we need a better understanding of what video games are and what they do to players. The games advertised in cinemas and on bus stops are only a small selection of what is available. The actual breadth of the possible experiences is hugely diverse and varied: from cancer to prayer, childhood abandonment to ecstatic worship of creation, and even the fleeting nature of life. These smaller games are rarely discovered because of their niche nature and being drowned out by the noise surrounding bigger blockbuster titles.

How games address these topics is different to other media. We know they are built from lines of code. They are spreadsheets that invite us to play a numbers game. This means that we can consider them more like machines than art. However, their mechanics address cultural themes much like films and novels. It's just that they do it in a unique way. Unlike books, video games don't tell stories or describe locations. Instead, they task players with discovering or overhearing narratives ongoing in their worlds. They invite players to explore and, at times, to lose themselves in the geography of the environments they create. Unlike films, video games don't always dictate what players see or direct their interpretation of a particular scene. Instead, they ask players to control their own point of view and construct their own sense of what is unfolding around them.

Video games create spaces that receive the player. Whether it's a simple puzzle or an expansive world, we are invited to go to another place. We are drawn into these spaces similarly to how the eye is drawn over a painting, only here, the world is moving too. These virtual spaces require human interaction to come alive. They don't unfold at a predetermined pace or in a premeditated direction. The game designer may have a story to tell, but has to let the player discover it at their own pace. Consequently, stories are not dictated, but overheard. Opportunities to discover a narrative are many within a game world, and will likely be encountered in a haphazard fashion. Some of this will be traditional narration or dialogue but equally, games tell stories with the worlds they create and how the player can (or can't) interact with different elements.

These two aspects of gaming spaces – that they require our presence and that they allow us to dictate how we progress – mean that they are co-owned between the developer and the player. At times it's hard to tell where the developer's intention ends and the influence of the player begins. In turn, this means that interpretation is intrinsic to video games. Even young players become expert at interpreting what is happening in the spaces that games create. This sense of ownership combines with other aspects of video game spaces – that they are unpredictable, exciting, personal, fragile, intimate, imaginative, raw and wild – to create a rich cocktail of potential for finding meaning in new ways.

Becoming a gamer

Discovering this aspect of video games for ourselves is essential to being able to guide young people and children towards healthy and enriching experiences. However, for those of us not used to playing, encountering a game can feel like drowning in a complex spreadsheet, with confusing calculations and an intimidating vastness. To move beyond this, video games require a new kind of literacy that, like any new language, isn't trivial to learn. Along with understanding how to move around, progress and read the clues provided by the game makers, video games have the added hurdle of requiring specific hardware and being controlled by unfamiliar devices. Games are also developing rapidly with augmented reality (AR) and virtual reality (VR) adding further challenges and opportunities.

As well as the advice in this chapter, you need to find a guide – ideally someone in your community or congregation who can help navigate beyond the commercial blockbuster games and regularly introduce gaming content that surprises, challenges and engages you. This can be time-consuming and difficult work, but is essential to understand the world of games that children and young people enjoy. It lays the groundwork for you to identify ways to be present in this world for your children's work. Of course, the side benefit is that, hopefully, you will discover games you personally benefit from along the way.

Being present

With this deeper understanding of gaming, and a commitment to discovering great games for ourselves, we can now consider how to incorporate digital play as an integral part of our work with children. Creating these sessions for your children and young people will be specific to your context. Find games you think are interesting and enjoyable experiences, or address topics that will engage those you work with. Consider their age and select games that are appropriate. This can be tricky if you don't have a wide knowledge of gaming, but again, time spent playing the games yourself and resources, like those I have listed at the end of this chapter, will help.

Give some thought to the physical space where you will play the game. It should be free from distractions and offer the whole group a chance to play and interact. Signposting that this is more than just entertainment by adjusting lighting, setting up chairs or even using candles and incense can be helpful. In a youth club context, players will drop in and out, so it's good to be on hand to have conversations with the young people before they move on. In a more devotional setting, like a youth or children's service, play the game throughout rather than stopping and playing at a particular point. Integrating other elements, like worship, Bible reading and communion, with the game play are essential if it is to be more than a novel aside.

Grant the group permission to explore and experiment with the game in their own way, rather than steering them to play it 'correctly'. Part of the benefit of video games is a relinquishing and sharing of control over how things proceed. Still, help the children notice what is happening in the game, and highlight aspects they might miss. Be ready with questions about what the game might be about and how it feels to play. Listen to the responses from the children as they play, as these are often enlightening and helpful to talk about further.

This approach enables us to expect more of the games we play together. Rather than incorporating video games into our current liturgy, we start to see them as spaces where we can discover and develop new ways of encountering God and exploring Christian spirituality that will grow with children and young people as they mature.

Examples that have worked well

The best way to illustrate this is with examples from my work with Dr Alastair Jones in this area in a variety of contexts. This includes the Christian arts festival Greenbelt, youth services, homegroups, the Lost Weekend festival in Exeter, Methodist minister training, sessions at secondary schools and Frontier Youth Trust (FYT) youth worker training workshops.

Alastair recently reflected on a session playing the game *Gone Home* with a youth group: 'I had some of the best conversations I've had with them about how parents relate to their children. This led to exploring how neither they nor their children are perfect.' He went on to highlight the ease with which these conversations occur:

Playing games with children and showing interest in their world is a natural space to connect on a deeper level and something they welcome. This helps children grow in their understanding of video games so they can establish language and the capacity to talk about their online world. It becomes a vital part of their spiritual formation that matures with them as they encounter more mature digital experiences.

It has taken us time to find the right games for these different contexts, and we haven't always got it right. The following examples are all games that have worked well with a range of age groups. I've arranged them with the best games for younger children first and the later examples are more suitable for older young people:

- *Proteus* (Windows, PlayStation (PS) 3, PS Vita): a simple game where players explore a pixelated island landscape. This works well for younger children who can have fun chasing digital rabbits or watching blocky dragonflies. They can take the experience at their own pace, noticing how their presence affects the world. The game will also develop as older players discover how to trigger different seasons and eventually leave the island.

- *Joust Mania* (Unix) and *Sports Friends* (PS3, PS4, Mac, PC): two versions of an electronic game of tag played with PS Move controllers. Up to 16 players each hold the motion-sensitive controller and try to keep it still while jostling to nudge each other. The screen isn't used at all and the controllers light up to indicate when players are knocked out. It's a lot of fun and creates discussions of how we interact with each other, the importance of teamwork and listening. Most of all, though, like any game, it creates a unique space in which children, young people and adults can interact.

- *Passage* (Web): available free online and very simple to play. It tracks a man through the course of his life. The novelty is that this is depicted in blocky graphics and the whole game takes just a few minutes to complete. Players make their way through the maze of the man's life and can watch him age in front of their eyes. With multiple playthroughs it creates a context for often moving and honest reflections on the meaning of life and the choices we make.

- *Space Team* (Android, iOS): a space piloting challenge. Up to six players connect to each other on their smartphones or tablets.

They must then follow instructions to press the spaceship's control buttons quickly enough to stop the ship crashing. The twist is that they only have instructions for the buttons on other players' screens. Players soon realise they have to communicate well to survive. On occasion I've discussed how this compares to the Tower of Babel narrative.

- *A Dark Room* (iOS, Android, Browser): an adventure entirely told with text. At first you can only stoke a fire and bring light and heat to the room. From here you progress through its five hours of gameplay by tiny increments – being able to build huts for strangers, venture out to the village and start to collect resources. As you do, an intriguing story slowly emerges that suggests all is not what it seems.

- *Journey* (PS3, PS4): a game where you explore a barren desert landscape. This reveals an ancient society and ruined temples. Other human players (online) will suddenly appear in the game. Although the players can't speak to each other, experts often help new players progress with a series of chirps and gestures. At the end of the game the player encounters a heavenly otherworld of light and tranquillity. I've used *Journey* in Exeter Cathedral for a communion service.

- *Bury Me My Love* (iOS, Android): a virtual companion that lives on your smartphone, tablet or PC. You play the role of a husband of a Syrian migrant, Nour, trying to get to Europe. Its text message adventure is played in real time, with Nour popping up with questions and updates at unexpected moments. Your answers, sometimes just an emoticon, affect Nour's decisions and journey. It takes a few days to complete and each play thought is different. The serious topic, the fact that Nour could die, and the amount of reading make this an excellent game for older teenagers.

- *That Dragon, Cancer* (iOS, Mac, PC): a game created by parents of a young child with terminal brain cancer. Suitable for older players, it uses family recordings and significant locations to tell the story of what it's like to face terminal illness as a parent. Where young people are mature enough to cope with the topic, it creates a space where prayer, healing and hope are addressed in a unique and moving way.

Untapped potential of video games

This chapter has dealt with the challenges and opportunities facing children and children's workers in the emerging world of video games. I've aimed to reframe things to move us from policing and promoting particular behaviour to creating a context in which children's gaming can flourish. The research is sobering, but also a good sanity check on the all-too-common knee-jerk reactions to horror stories circulated online and in tabloid newspapers. Although we are still only starting to understand video game neuro-activity, physical health and emotional and social wellbeing, there are clear learnings here.

Children need adults to be present in their gaming world, not only to guide their playing towards health, but also to challenge them to play better games. By equipping them to interpret games for themselves, we help them develop language and tools to include gaming as part of their spiritual formation as they mature. Children's workers, parents and carers who become genuinely embedded in the video game world have a unique opportunity to create space and time to unlock gaming's untapped payload of social, psychological, ethical and maybe even spiritual benefits for the lives of the children they work with.

QUESTIONS FOR REFLECTION AND DISCUSSION

• What have you learned about yourself from watching films or reading fiction? Could this happen with a video game?

• How could you challenge your children and young people to get more from the games they play?

• What topics would you like games to made about? Google your answer, because they probably already exist.

• What is the biggest barrier to using video games in your children's work, and how could you resolve that?

Online resources

Ask About Games safe gaming advice: www.askaboutgames.com

Common Sense Media game advice: www.commonsensemedia.org

ESRB (Entertainment Software Rating Board) game ratings and synopsis: www.esrb.org

Weekly video guides on games for youth workers and parents: www. patreon.com/geekdadgamer

PEGI (Pan European Game Information) game ratings and content overview: https://videostandards.org.uk

References and further reading

Byron, T. (2008) *Safer Children in a Digital World.* Available at http://webarchive.nationalarchives.gov. uk/20100202110916/http://www.dcsf.gov.uk/byronreview

Domoff, S.E., Harrison, K., Gearhardt, A.N., Gentile, D.A., Lumeng, J.C. and Miller, A.L. (2017) 'Development and validation of the Problematic Media Use Measure: A parent report measure of screen media "addiction" in children.' *Psychology of Popular Media Culture,* doi:10.1037/ ppm0000163

Ferguson, C.J. (2015) 'Does media violence predict societal violence? It depends on what you look at and when.' *Journal of Communication 65*(1), doi:10.1111/jcom.12129

Gentile, D.A., Li, D., Khoo, A., Prot, S. and Anderson, C.A. (2014) 'Mediators and moderators of long-term effects of violent video games on aggressive behavior: Practice, thinking, and action.' *JAMA Pediatrics 168*(5), 450–457.

Johnson, D., Jones, C., Scholes, L. and Colder Carras, M. (2013) *Videogames and Wellbeing: A Comprehensive Review.* Australia: Gaming Research Group – Young and Well Cooperative Research Centre.

Jones, A. and Robertson, A. (2017) *Exploring Spirituality in Video Games.* Cambridge: Grove Books.

Pryzbylski, A. (2017) 'Digital screen time limits and young children's psychological well-being: Evidence from a population-based study.' *Journal of Child Development,* doi:10.1111/cdev.13007

Pryzbylski, A. and Weinstein, N. (2017) 'Children's screen-time guidelines too restrictive, according to new research.' Available at www.ox.ac.uk/news/2017-12-14-children%E2%80%99s-screen-time-guidelines-too-restrictive-according-new-research

Shapiro, J. (2018) *Digital Play for Global Citizens.* Available at http://joanganzcooneycenter.org/wp-content/uploads/2018/03/jgcc_digitalplayforglobalcitizens.pdf

Chapter 7

EVENTS MANAGER
Big Dreams and Nuts and Bolts

Carolyn Edwards

Introduction

In Britain it appears that we have gone festival mad! There are food festivals, car festivals, flower festivals and, of course, famous and not so famous music festivals. Human beings like to gather and celebrate, find out about and experience – that's how God designed us! You only have to look at the calendar of festivals and feasts that he planned for the people of Israel set out in Leviticus 23 to realise that God loves a good gathering. The purpose of this chapter is to explore how we can plan and deliver gatherings and events that attract children to the Christian faith, and help them grow in their knowledge and love of God.

Envisioning and planning an event requires both big picture and small detail thinking. Any event that is organised needs to be part of a strategic plan, otherwise a lot of energy and resources can be wasted on something that might well have been 'good fun' or well attended but doesn't make the necessary connections or build relationships. But we also have to examine the minutiae. God loves the detail. Just take a look at the richness of the ritual in the Passover meal, and the instructions for the creation of the Tabernacle in Exodus 26 and then later the Temple passed on from David to Solomon in 1 Chronicles 28. It is important to have thought through a lot of the detail, and one helpful way is to imagine yourself as a participant, arriving without knowing anything about what is going to happen…how will you know where to go, what to take with you, when to be picked up, etc.?

In Acts 2.42–47 we see an attractional model of mission, where as more people turned to faith, so their lifestyle changed, and the loving and generous nature of their community drew people to it. In many ways our context is similar to that of the early Church, where Christianity was a minority religion. And in many ways it is different as there weren't perhaps so many distractions on offer, but it is worth thinking about whether we are expecting people to come and join in with what we already do, or whether we are offering new and relevant ways of engaging with the Christian faith. Pete Ward addresses some of these questions in his book, *Liquid Church*, and challenges us to consider how what was attractional because if offered refuge has become a resort where the idle can take a year-long vacation (Ward 2002, p.28).

Ask any marketing or management student and they will tell you there are three key questions that need to be considered for an effective strategy:

- Where are we now?

- Where do we want to be?

- How are we going to get there?

The same applies for event planning in the Church and children's work.

Where are we now?

To put on an event that really scratches the itch for your mission and ministry as well as the local population, it is worth taking a step back and considering what is really going on in your local community. What kind of reputation and connections does your church or organisation have? What events are already happening that it would be foolish to replicate? For instance, if the local sports centre always does a 'football camp', make sure your holiday club is in a different week. Spend some time gathering information before you decide what to do, not only about what is or is not happening locally, but also what has been done before (and whether it went well or not). In addition, consider what resources are realistically available in terms of people and money.

Where do we want to be?

The answer to this will depend on the answers to the first question. Yes, what we want is for every child in our town/village to know and love Jesus, but sometimes that's a goal we never quite reach, and knowing where we are will help us to plan what the next step should be. In 2004 the Lausanne Forum put together the Pattaya Scale as a visual means of helping individuals and congregations develop effective mission and discipleship of children. It illustrates how a child could move from no understanding of the Gospel at all through to an active missional ministry of their own. The important starting place for any event is asking, what

are we trying to achieve? Do we want to put the church on the map –
raise awareness of its existence in the local community? Or at the other
end of the spectrum, do we want the children we are working with to
learn and experience something new of the God they know and how
to live for him?

Below in Table 7.1 is by no means an exhaustive list, but some helpful
suggestions on the kind of events that could work for different strategic
aims.

TABLE 7.1: EVENT OPTIONS FOR DIFFERENT PURPOSES

Purpose	Event	Description
Raising awareness in the community	History day	Dig around and find out if your church has something interesting in it or a link with a famous historical character. Link up with the local history society and open the doors for visitors to find out more, enjoy a vintage tea shop and themed activities
	Parenting fair	Pull together local support agencies, provide uniform exchange and children's activities, while parents get helpful information
Making connections	Light party	Halloween is becoming big business. Offer an alternative, where children still get the opportunity to dress up and eat far too much sugar, but where the theme is light and hope rather than darkness and fear. Scripture Union offers a free pack to help you organise one of these
	Sports or arts club	Many children have completely overwhelming after-school activities timetables. Many don't. What are the needs in your community, and how can you provide sports sessions or opportunities to be creative for children who would not otherwise have them?
	Family Fun Day	In long holidays many parents and carers are desperate to find things that will entertain their children for not a lot of money. If you don't have the resources to put on a whole week of holiday club, a couple of mornings of activities can help you get to know the local children and build confidence and enthusiasm in your church
	After-school club	Many schools are under immense pressure to offer wrap-around care for pupils, particularly those where parents are working long hours. This takes resources that many don't have, but which the church could provide. It is a big commitment because you need to staff it every term-time week day, and you need to be sensitive and agree with the school what kind of Christian content, if any, is allowed, but it can be an excellent way of making connections with the community

Building relationships	Holiday club	This is still a popular way of engaging with children who don't normally come to church. In Buckinghamshire, many churches gather together to provide all-day activities for hundreds of children through the Lighthouse holiday club, but don't be put off if five mornings are all you can manage. If this is the first time you have done a holiday club, it is a good idea to use a published resource as a starting point, even if you have to amend it to make it work for your context
	Monthly club	Whether you want to keep contact with the children and families who came to your parent-and-toddler group now that they have gone to school, or those who came to your fun day or holiday club, a monthly club at the church means that you are maintaining that relationship without the resource commitment of a weekly club. If your church has the facilities, consider providing a simple hot meal as part of the club to help out parents who don't necessarily have the means or time to provide this
	Messy Church	Although it could be argued that this is the same as monthly club with a meal, I have put this separately, as Lucy Moore, who came up with the concept of Messy Church, is adamant that the key word is 'Church'. Some 'Messy Church' activities have degenerated into craft clubs. If you want to do a craft club, then do one, but as a church you need to decide whether Messy Church is a better form of outreach, and strategically what you are going to do about this congregation as it develops
Discipling	All-night prayer and praise	There is something very exciting about sleeping on a church hall floor with a bunch of mates, but don't underestimate the heart many children have for praying and praising (see the 'Children Can' material for more on how to facilitate children as prayer and praise warriors[1])
	Weekend/ week away	A great opportunity for more intensive teaching and intentional discipleship through 24/7 (well that's what it feels like!) interaction. For longer events encourage the children to attend camps organised by national organisations like Scripture Union or CPAS. In this way they will meet and make friends with other Christians from around the country, which can have a really positive impact on their faith
	Mission trip	Your church may have links with missionaries or mission agencies around the world. Is there an opportunity for you to take a group of children to help with a specific project or activity? This has to be thought through very carefully, and much better done as a family activity, not just because of the logistical considerations of visas and vaccinations, etc., but appropriately exposing children to the realities of different cultures

1   https://www.childrencan.co.uk

Once you have some answers to the question of 'Where do we want to be?', you can start asking questions about what you think God wants to communicate through this particular event. For some children a summer holiday club may be their only contact with church throughout the year; think carefully about how to use themes and Bible stories that maintain continuity over the years, but also are not too repetitive, and introduce Old and New Testament elements. What characteristics of God do you want to share during your event? How can you keep the interest of regular church attenders with stories from the Bible they may not be so familiar with, while also communicating the nuts and bolts of the Christian faith to those who know nothing?

How are we going to get there?

Many of your potential volunteers work full time in the 'real world' and will measure your preparation and communication by those they are used to at work. Sloppiness and unprofessionalism will put them off really getting behind your venture. Use the skills of those around you – if they are good at putting together budgets, let them do that. If they are creative and want to develop some interesting craft ideas, let them do that. If they like hunting around online for bargain rates for bouncy castles, leave them to it!

Having said that, be prepared to do your bit as part of the team. I grew up as part of a family that ran Christian camps for children. Every summer, our whole household, including the dog, would move out to a field in Sussex for just over four weeks, joined by hundreds of children and willing volunteers. It was a basic site with everything under canvas, and portaloos that required emptying every day. One day as a young teenager I caught my dad trundling up the field with a toilet bucket in each hand. I asked why he hadn't left this job for someone else in the team to do. His explanation – that he wasn't going to ask anyone in the team to do something he wasn't prepared to do himself – revolutionised my understanding of leadership. As a leader we cannot do everything; we do need to delegate for tasks to get done efficiently and effectively, but we must also be prepared to model the servant leadership of Jesus, washing feet or carrying buckets of excrement as required.

Nuts and bolts

Be happy!

When you gather don't just think about the functionality of what you are doing; consider how joyful and united your gathering looks to those who are watching from the sidelines – from parents who deliver children right through to the caretakers of the property you are using. Try to eat together and do something, either as part of your planning and training day or the event itself, that is designed to bless, encourage and bring joy to those who have given up time to make the event a success. It could be something as simple as a packet of donuts, but I firmly believe that good events run on the Holy Spirit and the tea urn, so don't stint on providing good quality refreshments for your volunteers.

Money

Communicate costs to punters. If you are going to need to charge for refreshments, make sure the information says 'refreshments on sale', so that people come with money.

Registration

If you are running a family event, make it clear to parents and carers that the children remain their responsibility. It is still worth having a signing in sheet including name, number of people and contact email (so that they can be told about the next event), so that you have a list to work from in case of an emergency.

If the children are going to be left with you, you must have a completed registration form with:

- the child's name, address and date of birth

- health information (e.g. allergies, inhalers and additional needs)

- emergency contact details

- arrangements for pick up

- permission for emergency first aid and taking of photographs.

It is always a good idea to have at least one team member dedicated to collecting correctly completed forms, compiling a register and checking the number of children against that register. If you are expecting a large number of children (30+), it is a good idea to offer pre-registration so that the registration queue does not get too long. The reality is that many parents don't do this, so be prepared on the first morning with extra volunteers to help the process run more smoothly. Make sure you also understand and comply with the latest requirements of the General Data Protection Regulation (in force from May 2018).

Additional needs

If a child arrives at the event with medical equipment (most usually inhalers or epipens), agree with the child, parent and person who will have responsibility for the child at the event where it will be kept, and how and when it should be used. You should have a first aider as part of your team who is trained in administering epipens, etc., but it is as well for other team members to be aware of any possible symptoms, and protocols they need to be aware of. Some parents of children with medical conditions are very anxious about leaving them, which often gets passed on to the children. The more informed you are and able to offer clear systems and experienced individuals to deal with additional needs, the more confident the parent can be, and the more likely the child is to settle quickly.

Food allergies are a significant issue, so think carefully about how you can be inclusive and also cater for those you wish to protect. One holiday club I ran that had a long morning session, in which the children required a mid-morning snack to keep them going, changed from offering biscuits to fruit. Not only did this protect my son who is anaphylactic to wheat, but it also meant that it was healthier for everyone! When you are making these decisions, do, however, bear in mind the cost and time factor. Another event I lead where there are over 100 children asks parents to provide children with a mid-morning snack. This reduces the cost, but does mean every morning there are tears from somebody who has forgotten to bring theirs, or whose parents didn't read the polite notice and have brought a snack with nuts in. Back-up snacks are provided, but this can have an enormous impact on a child who is already feeling slightly overwhelmed.

Many events can be high octane noise and activity, which is why so many children enjoy it, but not all, so make sure you put space and time for reflection in your programme too. It is also good to be prepared for children with additional educational and social needs, by providing a quiet space in your venue where children can withdraw from noise and activity if they are feeling overwhelmed. Again, it is really important to talk to the child and their grown-ups about what helps them feel safe and content, and what should be avoided.

Planning a session

It is always good to have a plan, and to have an idea of how long different elements of your session will take. Sometimes children do an activity that you have spent endless hours preparing, in seconds. Sometimes what you thought would be a five-minute activity can take three times as long. Be realistic in your timings. Read the story you are going to tell really quickly and really slowly to get a feel for how long it might take. Make the craft using one hand or with no scissors (there are never enough scissors on the craft table!) to see how long the children with weaker fine motor skills will take to complete it. Remember, if you are putting small groups in different rooms and then bringing them together for upfront time that it can take an age gathering everyone, so have some simple hand games ready to play with the children who arrived at the first call. Design flexibility into the programme with back-up activities to fill an unexpected space, or elements that you can drop if something else takes too long. Make sure you let the team know where these flexibilities are, and if you are using a large venue, try to give small group leaders five-minute warnings, so that they can move the group along.

What you are able to do in a session will depend largely on the venue, and the size and capability of your team. It is tempting, particularly if you are gifted, to keep things 'upfront' with one person or a small team 'entertaining' the children, but this is not where real relationships are built, or where children are able to articulate their questions and expressions of faith. The role of small group leader is challenging because they have to facilitate a group of children who might never have been together before through a variety of activities. Where possible double up, and for an inexperienced team make sure there is thorough training beforehand and daily briefing and debriefing.

Don't under-estimate the part that the children and young people can play in ministering and evangelising to each other. If you cannot include children as part of your planning team, make sure you use them as a sounding board. Encourage them to pray for the event and those who are going to be coming. Consider how they can participate in the teaching and communication. For more information on how to encourage children in exercising spiritual gifts and praying for each other, etc., see material produced by Powerpack[2] and Children Can.[3]

When working on ideas, remember to draw inspiration from both the Bible and your theme. It is easy to get carried away with 'under the

2   www.powerpackministries.co.uk
3   www.childrencan.co.uk

sea' or 'superheroes' or whatever the latest thing is and end up stretching biblical material to fit. This is where a well-thought-out answer to the question 'What one thing do we want the children to take home with them?' can help to keep you focused, as you can then shape any worship and teaching, fun and games around helping them to hear and digest that one thing.

Children learn and engage in a variety of ways, so make sure you use a variety of ways for communicating. Marlene LeFever's book *Learning Styles* is a helpful resource for thinking about the four key ways that children assimilate learning and learn. Most children are visual, but many also need to time to think and process what they have heard and seen. Don't be frightened of putting times of quiet and stillness in your programme. Some children might need coaching through it, because many are not familiar with silence and stillness, but with the right environment and guidelines most children relax into it very quickly, and relish the opportunity to dwell in God's presence in ways they don't often get the chance to.

Having fun for no purpose other than to have fun is important. Don't underestimate the power of laughter (see the chapter entitled 'Poo, bum, willy' in my book *Slugs and Snails and Puppy Dogs' Tails* for the impact humour can have on our spirituality), but think carefully about the balance of teaching, worship, activity and general silliness as well as watching, doing, thinking and feeling. If you are doing a regular event, or one that lasts a few days, consider what elements of structure and repetition you can put in to help the children, and in particular, those on the autism spectrum, feel secure.

Boundaries

It is also really important that the team and participants know what the rules are, and that these are applied consistently (see also Chapter 12 later in this book). Make sure you regularly review and communicate your safeguarding policy so that everyone is reminded of what is appropriate and how to ensure that they can demonstrate effective Christian love to the children (and this includes appropriate touch) without fear of misinterpretation.

One of the biggest challenges of running any activity with children is getting enough volunteers. The NSPCC recommend the following ratios:

- 0–2 years: 1 adult to 3 children

- 2–3 years: 1 adult to 4 children

- 4–8 years: 1 adult to 6 children
- 9–12 years: 1 adult to 8 children
- 13–18 years: 1 adult to 10 children.

This means that you might have to limit numbers, but if that is the case, make sure you communicate that as much as possible beforehand, and stress that this is for the children's benefit.

One way of ensuring you have enough volunteers (and demonstrating the attractional quality of ecumenical unity discussed earlier in this chapter) is to put on an event with other churches. Sometimes this is more easily done through a para-church organisation like the Scripture Union Xcite events, but as long as you have a representative from each church involved, it can work. Work with the strengths of each congregation. One church may have a lot of storage space but cannot provide many volunteers; another may not have many who are able to work with children, but they can provide great cakes to keep the team going. Be aware of potential doctrinal differences, particularly around communion and infant baptism, and ensure when you are communicating that you do not assume that your understanding is always the right one! Be prepared for the inevitable time lag. Working with one church can sometimes feel like walking through treacle, as proposals need to be approved by various committees; now multiply that by a number of churches and denominations! It is not unrealistic to expect the planning of a large ecumenical project to take a year to come to fruition.

QUESTIONS FOR REFLECTION AND DISCUSSION

- What is the main purpose of the event(s) you do, and how do they fit in to your strategic vision?
- How much are you expecting the children and families in your neighbourhood to conform to traditional patterns of engagement with the Church? What can you do that is different?
- How can you plan for contingencies including changes in team, funding and location?

Online resources

The NSPCC has some useful advice on safeguarding, etc.: www.nspcc.org

The Pattaya Scale: www.aimlower.com/wp-content/uploads/The-Pattaya-Scale.pdf

Powerpack has some useful information on enabling children in prayer ministry, etc.: www.powerpackministries.co.uk

References and further reading

Edwards, C. (2011) *Slugs and Snails and Puppy Dogs' Tails: Helping Boys Connect to God.* Leicester: IVP (Inter-Varsity Press).

Goldenberg, O. (2011) *The Josiah Generation.* East Malling, ME: River Publishing & Media. (Children Can).

LeFever, M. (2009) *Learning Styles.* Eastbourne: Kingsway.

Thompson, H. (2012) *Ignite: A Resource for Equipping Leaders of Children's Ministry.* Powerpack Ministries.

Moore, L. and Leadbetter, J. (2017) *Messy Church.* Leicester: IVP (Inter-Varsity Press).

Ward, P. (2002) *Liquid Church.* Milton Keynes: Paternoster Press.

Chapter 8

HOODIE

Spiritual Direction, Silence and Prayer

Barbara Meardon

The hoodie

Imagine two very different hood-wearing people – a teenager walking down the street wearing a hoodie passing a monk wearing a monastic hood and habit. I wonder what they would be thinking; I wonder what others would be thinking. What we wear can affect our reception in society, in our jobs, in schools and in places of worship. Although hoodies have a 3000-year history (Antonelli 2018), many teenagers are stereotyped as misbehaving members of a community when they are seen wearing a hoodie. Indeed, Hertsmere Young Researchers found that 'negative reporting causes a greater fear of the issue than the actual reality of the reported problem and enhances stereotyping. Imbalanced negative portrayal of young people in the media has a damaging effect on young people and the community in which they live' (2011, p.4). Hoods (or hoodies) can serve as:

- a form of protection

- a means of covering or altering one's visibility

- a means of representation (including a form of expression and/or fashion).

In a blog, 'On hoods and hoodies: A theological reflection', Tomi Oredein (2012) writes that 'The monks' clerical hood and the hooded sweatshirt or hoodie both speak a particular and peculiar message, but often this message is read on multiple levels, whether the wearer intends for it to be or not.' Despite the controversy surrounding the hoodie and 'ban-a-hoodie' headlines, especially at the turn of the century, people from all backgrounds have embraced the hoodie. Zara Phillips, a member of the British royal family, has included hoodies in her range of equestrian clothing, and Facebook CEO Mark Zuckerberg often wears a plain grey hoodie rather than a business suit. Can these modern hoodie wearers learn anything from the traditional hood-wearing monk that will help them cope with the fast-changing, noisy, tech-filled multi-tasking reality of their lives, and can the Church facilitate that?

'In the world but not of it...': Monks and nuns

Ian Adams suggests that wherever we are there are patterns from monastic tradition that can be adapted to help us change the world for the better (2010). With many monks and nuns living set apart in a consecrated place in a structured, secluded community with rules for living a common way of life, Lambert (2012) offers two reasons why following the example of nuns and monks is a good idea in a busy world. Brain scans by neuroscientists on Franciscan Sisters of Christian Charity have shown that meditative, mindful and contemplative practices change the brain for the better. People are drawn to the benefits of such a life – he cites the 40,000 hits on Worth Abbey's website following the BBC-broadcast *The Monastery* programme in May 2005, following five men who spent 40 days in a contemplative way of life.

Rather than cloistered life in a monastery, I find the pattern of the Irish monks like Saint Columba a more helpful pattern for those trying to live in the world but not of it. McCarthy (2007) writes that these *perigrini* (Latin for 'pilgrims'), 'the Celtic monks, chose to pursue both godliness and engagement with their world. They did not retreat. They engaged and transformed their world.' Growing up in the North East of England, and especially as a teenager, I was very influenced and inspired myself by the lives of the Celtic saints and the experiences of pilgrimage to Lindisfarne and Durham. I was surprised when I moved to a different part of the country and found that this was not a usual formation journey for young people.

The new monasticism movement of the twenty-first century suggests translating the spirituality of the great monastic traditions (such as the Benedictines or the Franciscans) into the world of today, and includes patterns of community and pilgrimage. They take different forms but have common patterns; for example, in *New Celtic Monasticism for Everyday People* Ray Simpson (2005) talks about a common way of life and includes a 'Way for Living for Young People', which gives ten simple guidelines for living (see the end of this chapter, 'Resources for spiritual practices'), something similar to a 'Rule of Life'.[1] The increasingly popular

---

1   www.northumbriacommunity.org/who-we-are/our-rule-of-life/what-is-a-rule-of-life

pilgrimage to Santiago de Compostela in Spain is called 'The Camino', which translates as 'The Way': Christianity began as a way of life. Jesus said that he is 'the Way' (John 14.6), and the earliest Christians were known as 'followers of the Way'. David Runcorn (2006), in his *Spirituality Workbook*, writes about a community without walls inspired by the German theologian Dietrich Bonhoeffer (1906–1945): 'Even in the midst of society facing powerful evil and in deep moral and spiritual confusion, Bonhoeffer still insisted that Christian community is to be lived in the midst of it all – without walls' (2006, p.56).

Children and young people now

Many believe that children and young people today face a worrying combination of moral and spiritual confusion. The Children's Society's *The Good Childhood Report* (2017, p.5) found that 'one million teenagers have seven or more serious problems in their lives. At a time of drastic Government cuts to funding for local children's services, the findings give deep cause for concern.' Palmer (2007), in *Toxic Childhood*, referring to Martin Lindstrom's book *BRANDchild* (2004), states 'as formal religion in the Western world continues to erode, brands move in to fill the vacuum' (2007, p.241), and writes about how shocked she is that children's play has been invaded by consumerism.

Although many children and young people do not attend church, they are not the secular generation that was predicted in the 1960s, along with the death of Christianity and other religions. Contemporary Western culture is largely post-secular. While there may be a significant decline in conventional organised religion as such, there is still widespread belief in the sacred and an acknowledgement that we are spiritual. This generation, however, are largely unchurched, so although they have innate spirituality and are open to exploring that, the traditions and practices of the Church or other faith communities are largely unfamiliar to many of them. Even children and young people who go to church may have largely experienced separate-from-adult programmes and had little opportunity to experience the kind of worship and spiritual practices such as silent prayer or meditation that are part of old and new monasticism. Westerhoff (2012) is concerned that in both society and the Church, 'the rituals of society are taken more seriously than those of the church and we are more influenced by them' (2012, p.78). Runcorn writes about an 'underlying longing for spiritual life that is evident in the profusion of alternative therapies, spiritualities and meditation techniques on offer' that should be taken seriously, and finds that 'the historic riches of Christian spirituality are as relevant as they have ever been' (2006, p.1).

Why does this matter? In his book *Will Our Children Have Faith?* Westerhoff states that, 'for faith it is especially important to acknowledge that the most significant and fundamental form of learning is experience' (2012, p.61). The church must share the experience of spiritual practices with children and young people as a counter-cultural way of living.

Spirituality in contemporary culture: how, where and when can children and young people learn these things in the Church today?

First, children and young people want to be welcomed and to belong, and like to take part in rituals even when they don't understand them. I found in teaching that children who had never attended or visited church had the most amazing experiences when I included candles in a reflection or wondering time, and experienced a moment of joy myself when one non-church four-year-old boy exclaimed, 'I'd sing to God of the universe' when asked what he would talk to God about.

Children need the companioning and supervision of adults, models and mentors, relationships and connectedness. Children need exposure to ideas that will stretch them and feed their curiosity. They need to hear adults talking about things they don't always quite understand. Barnett (2015) uses the term 'alongsiding' as well as modelling. I find this a most helpful term that church leaders and volunteers alike have found instantly explains our role in working with children and young people and their families. We are called to be alongside as well as to model, to share in the journey of spiritual development and experience as 'alongsiders', not as leaders who will tell children and young people the answers but as fellow seekers. 'Alongsiding' encapsulates this change in dynamic in children and young people's work in the church.

Spiritual practices and 'alongsiding' opportunities for experiential development

Within services, meetings, children and young people's groups

As Westerhoff states, 'We live as Christians when we discern what God is doing in the world and join in his work. Worship should inspire and motivate us for such radical action' (2012, p.4). If you are thinking that the children and young people you work with can't be quiet or still, take courage from Runcorn's words in his *Spirituality Workbook*: 'Contemplative prayer has too often been regarded as something for spiritual specialists.

But rather than involving the mastery of spiritual techniques it begins with nothing more than a capacity for wonder' (2006, p.183). Children are so good at wondering and being contemplative when given the opportunity and the tools, and can be great teachers too. Jesus tells grown-ups to learn from that childlike quality (Mark 10.13–16).

Runcorn (2006) explains that liturgy is scaffolding. It offers a protective shape for our praying, providing a safe structure for the building up of our prayer and worship. Liturgy holds our praying in a shape it needs to mature and deepen, and regularity soaks into us and is memorable. This should apply to all work with children and young people. They can use or hear words they don't understand but still be moved by them. Here are some ways that I have found offer good opportunities for doing that.

- *Quiet or silent prayer.* Children from a young age can be taught to hold and appreciate short periods of silence. One of the best ways I have found of doing this is by using bubble prayers. Talk to the children about what you are going to pray for, for example, giving thanks for God's wonderful creation all around us or praying for people they know. Ask the children to name the thing or person they are praying for. Ask them to choose one bubble and watch it as it floats away until it pops, and when it pops, ask them to say 'Amen'. The effect of this will be to have silence followed by lots of 'Amens' as the bubbles pop in succession, leading to a wonderful shared prayer experience.

  For older children having some quiet music can support an introduction to pausing and being quiet, but it is important to work towards silence. When you begin a session pause, be quiet – perhaps light a candle as a signal for a quieter time. If you set a reflective task such as rewriting a Psalm that talks of silence, for example, Psalm 131, 'I have calmed and quieted my soul', try to spread everyone out so that they are in their own quiet space to think and listen to themselves and God. Some children find it easier to be doing something quietly like drawing or creating something, but others would rather just be quiet. Offer choices so that they know that there is more than one way to be quiet and still.

- *Reflective storytelling* in the style of *Godly Play* or Trevor Cooling's (2011) excellent *Storybags* books gives lots of space for quiet storytelling, silence and wondering. These work with all ages and in intergenerational settings where adults and young people can learn from children about reflection, particularly when that hasn't been their previous experience in church. With teenagers I have found that using something like the *NOOMA* films, which are characterised by the quiet reflective wondering style of Rob Bell, is a helpful introduction to a discussion of how our faith interacts with our experience in the world.

The more you practise, the better it gets. In my experience children and young people find silence easier and indeed, helpful and enriching. It becomes very important that when they are in intergenerational settings they are seeing that this is something adults do too. My favourite example of where this doesn't happen is when adults in the congregation lead intercessions. They frequently invite people to think of their own prayers or people who need prayer in the silence, but move straight on without it. I find myself silently pleading, hang on, I've only just started forming my thoughts, and you didn't allow me to pray them. There are other opportunities in worship where silence can be introduced, for example, at the end of sermons or readings, to quietly reflect on what's been said. If children and young people don't see silence and quiet being modelled, they are unlikely to see it as an important practice in faith development. Faith is caught rather than taught.

- Using *music* can be another way to 'be still and know that I am God' (Psalm 46.10). Patterns such as those at the Taizé and Iona communities have drawn hundreds and thousands of young people to enjoy the way of life and reflective meditative worship, and have produced easy-to-sing reflective music. But you can also use other church or secular music, again, being of the world but not part of it. Of course, the opposite is true; if your church only uses loud, fast music in its worship, especially with children and young people, there is no opportunity for them to experience stillness or quiet in their worship.

- *Meditation and mindfulness* are for Christians too. I have found both to be very successful tools to use with children and young people. Lambert (2012) suggests, however, that:

> Christian related concepts such as watchfulness and Christian contemplative practices like the slow meditative reading of Scripture known as *Lectio Divina*, practicing the presence of God, prayers such as the Jesus Prayer, biblical meditation, silence and solitude have not [been] featured in the market-place, and this new

cultural quest for interior freedom is only on the periphery of the Church's awareness.

It shouldn't be. Watchfulness, attentive hearing and seeing are an integral part of the Gospel Jesus taught.

- Again, *modelling* is key, talking about the benefits you have found and trying it so they experience it themselves. There are many good examples of Christian meditation and mindfulness online. The Mindful Christian has a number of meditations including for starting the day or learning to meditate. Loyola Press has three-minute retreats and D365 has daily pauses online (see the end of this chapter).

- *Services you might not expect children or young people to value or enjoy.* I have been amazed at the response from teenagers when introduced to the quieter services like Compline (Night Prayer). I have found that young people often say this is their favourite part of sleepovers or pilgrimages. They naturally connect to the idea of the liturgy being old and new at the same time, being repeated through time and around the world, part of a continuum of quiet worship.

- *Retreats: Half-day, day-long or longer.* Having had encouraging responses to quiet times in services, reflective storytelling and so on, I wrote a children's retreat day, *Let the Flame Burn Brighter*, with Sandra Millar. Although people might wonder whether a quiet day for such children is either appropriate or possible, within the Roman Catholic tradition, and also within other expressions of faith, children do take part in retreats, fasting, meditation and prayer. With this in mind, we decided to create such a day for children and adults together.

  Going on retreat has long been recognised as being beneficial for adults. Adults define it as going away from their usual environment to a specific place to be alone with God in a 'more silent and focused' way, often in a Christian monastic setting. The children's quiet day includes elements that adults who have been on retreat would recognise: silence, liturgy in chapel, subdued music, visual elements, leadership by a spiritual director, solitude, group discussion and reflection on the Bible. The experience is designed to allow children to explore being reflective Christians and to try out spiritual practices that they may not have experienced before. The activities include both verbal and non-verbal elements designed to help both children and adults use all their senses and imagination in exploring their faith.

Each section of the day is introduced by making connections to the children's own experience; for example, when exploring God taking care of Elijah's physical needs, this care is illustrated by emptying a bag of everyday objects from home. A choice of responses is offered, including quiet reflection and creative activities, because such open-ended experiences engage children. We trialled this at a local retreat house with a mixed group of eight- to eleven-year-olds from different churches. This was not a silent day, but a day with designated times of not talking; silence was expected in all corridors and gardens, and quiet in the activity rooms where music played softly in the background to enable a comfortable space and framework. The chapel times and mealtimes were a time of response and conversations. In spite of being told by a senior church leader that a children's retreat was an oxymoron, the results exceeded Sandra's and my expectations, with all the children engaging immediately, enjoying the silence and quiet and wanting to repeat the experience in the future. Feedback from the trial included: 'A brilliant day'; 'Perfect'; 'I liked it because I could connect with God.'

- *Pilgrimage.* N.T. Wright suggests that 'pilgrimage to holy places, though neither necessary nor sufficient for Christian living', offers to many 'a time of real growth and depth in discipleship', and a 'stimulus and an invitation to prayer' (2014, p.127). Following my own pilgrimage to Santiago de Compostela I created and co-led a number of 'teenagers and adults together' pilgrimages at Easter. These were mostly over five days, but one was a single day. Each was based on a story – Moses, Abraham and Sarah, the Road to Emmaus and St Aldhelm. The equal numbers of adults (including students) and teenagers ensured we were journeying together, 'alongsiding' each other, experiencing and sharing. The longer time away gave opportunities to develop a rhythm to each day and evening, with many moments for mindful walking, silent walking, prayer, storytelling and conversation.

Everyone who took part felt that Easter was a more powerful time following time aside from the normal busyness of life. Twice the pilgrimage ended with the Maundy Thursday washing of the feet, which was transformed by the presence of pilgrims having their feet washed, and certainly introduced the young people to a quiet service they wouldn't normally attend, ending with the symbolic stripping of the altar. Mobile phones were not allowed, although the young people knew they could use an adult's phone to ring home if needed. Leaders only used phones for safety or urgent use. No young person complained about this, and many of us felt liberated by the break from technology. A small group of the adults, students and young people subsequently chose to walk part of the pilgrimage to Santiago de Compostela. Gatta (2016, p.93) reminds us that, 'given our nature and evolutionary history, we still need on occasion to make our way in the world mindfully by foot. For the health of both soul and body we must still walk, must walk often and with gratitude, even or especially in this age of supersonic transport and instantaneous communication.'

With younger children and older adults a shorter walk or pilgrimage might be easier to start with and could be done on a Sunday, inviting the whole congregation and all ages, if the route is chosen carefully. Include some of the spiritual practices mentioned above as you start and end your journey, and perhaps a stop or two in the middle. Explain before you go what will happen and what's expected, for example, no mobile phones to be used, walk consciously, notice what's around you and your breathing, use all your senses, everyone stop and listen for a while, what do you hear? Walk in silence for a given length of time, pray for people or places as you pass or pause. Break bread together. Share experiences, feelings, thoughts and prayers at the end... ask 'I wonder' questions so everyone knows there is no right or wrong answer/thought. As Adams notes, 'It seems to me that the traveling band of disciples has much to offer us as a picture of a religious community taking seriously its call to both seek after God and to be engaged with the wider world' (2010, p.35).

Final thoughts

According to Westerhoff, 'More difficult is how to live faithfully as resident aliens in a post-Christian era. We will need to find a new way of being-in-but-not-of-the-world while we avoid being-in-and-of-the-world' (2012, p.137). If the Church can share spiritual practices and alongside them on the way, I believe that children and young people and the adults will learn from each other, understand more about each other, and be better equipped for the journey.

QUESTIONS FOR REFLECTION AND DISCUSSION

- What or who has been most influential in your faith journey?

- What are the important things of church and faith we should share with children?

- What experiences do children and young people need to have had to equip them for a life of faith?

- I wonder what you assume when you see a hooded young person or a hooded monk – what judgements do you make or what might they remind you of?

- How could you include the experience of spiritual practices in the work your church does with children and young people?

Resources for spiritual practices

Back2School, D365, Pause Listen Think Go, a website with daily reflections: http://d365.org/de

Dorothy. C. Bass and Don C. Richter, with Lani Wright and Susan Briehl (2002) *Way to Live Leader's Guide, Ideas for Growing in Christian Practices with Teens*, Available at: https://practicingourfaith.org/pdf/WTL-LG_110504.pdf

Loyola Press, 3-minute retreats: www.loyolapress.com/3-minute-retreats-daily-online-prayer/about-3minute-retreats

Ray Simpson (2005) *New Celtic Monasticism for Everyday People*, pp.329–330. A Way for Living for Young People: Way 1: Discover Something; Way 2: Journey with a Soul Friend; Way 3: Make a Pattern; Way 4: Overcome; Way 5: Care for Animals an Earth; Way 6: Create a Good Lifestyle; Way 7: Mend what is Broken; Way 8: Join an Adventure; Way 9: Make Friends; Way 10: Share.

Rob Bell NOOMA videos: www.youtube.com/channel/UCYDYRgES_kLL60rz9utN2FA

Ten Simple Spiritual Practice Ideas for Children & Youth: http://gbod-assets.s3.amazonaws.com/legacy/kintera-files/about-gbod/UR_10SimpleSpiritualPractices.pdf

The Mindful Christian: www.themindfulchristian.net

Reflective storytelling

Cooling, M. (2011) *Bible Storybags*. Abingdon: Barnabas.

Godly Play: www.godlyplay.uk

Camps and residentials

Breathe*: The ethos behind Breathe* is to engage both body and soul. Young people are provided with space to rediscover some of the ancient Christian traditions of prayer and meditation, in a relevant and contemporary way: www.breatheyouthretreat.co.uk

Hilfield Youth Camp takes place every August at Hilfield Anglican Franciscan Friary in Dorset, UK. Organised by experienced volunteers, the camp offers up to 60 young people aged 13 to 17 the chance of a low-cost, fun holiday in stunning surroundings, while exploring a Christian theme. The camp is built on friendship, community and faith: www.hilfieldyouthcamp.org/Welcome.html

The Open Cloister's ministry is especially focused on providing the space and time for young people and young adults to retreat in a welcoming place where they can step away from everyday life and explore their spirituality, with the guidance of the Benedictine monastic community at Worth Abbey, in a calm, supportive and peaceful environment: https://worth.co.uk/retreats/young-people

Young Meditators is a programme of activities designed to help young adults find a community of peers who also meditate or who are interested Christian contemplation, with monthly retreats and seminars: http://wccm.org/content/young-meditators

References and further reading

Adams, I. (2010) *Cave Refectory Road*. Norwich: Canterbury Press.

Antonelli, P. (2018) 'Ted Talk on Hoodies.' Available at www.ted.com/talks/paola_antonelli_the_3_000_year_history_of_the_hoodie

Barnett, B. (2015) *All-age Worship*. Available at www.premier.org.uk/Topics/Church/Worship/All-age-Worship

Children's Society, The (2017) *The Good Childhood Report, Summary*. Available at www.childrenssociety.org.uk/what-we-do/resources-and-publications/the-good-childhood-report-2017

Gatta, J. (2016) 'Toward a Theology of Pilgrimage.' Available at www.baylor.edu/content/services/document.php/270260.pdf

Hertsmere Young Researchers (2011) 'Unbalanced negative media portrayal of youth.' April. Available at www.hertsmere.gov.uk/Documents/08-Parks--Leisure/Children--Young-People/Final-Report---Unbalanced-negative-media-portrayal-of-youth.pdf

Lambert, S. (2012) 'Being still in a busy world.' Evangelical Alliance, 22 June. Available at www.eauk. org/church/stories/being-still-in-a-busy-world.cfm

Lindstrom, M. (2004) *BRANDchild: Remarkable Insights into the Minds of Today's Global Kids and Their Relationship with Brands.* London: Kogan Page Limited.

McCarthy, D. (2007) 'Hearts and minds aflame for Christ: Irish monks – A model for making all things new in the 21st century.' *In Pursuit of Truth: A Journal of Christian Scholarship*, 28 September. Available at www.cslewis.org/journal/hearts-and-minds-aflame-for-christ-irish-monks—a-model-for-making-all-things-new-in-the-21st-century/view-all

Oredein, T. (2012) 'On hoods and hoodies: A theological reflection on clerical hoods, KKK hoods and the hoodie.' Blog. Available at https://tomioredein.wordpress.com/tag/hoodie

Palmer, S. (2007) *Toxic Childhood.* London: Orion Books.

Runcorn, D. (2006) *Spirituality Workbook.* London: SPCK.

Simpson, R. (2005) *A Pilgrim Way: New Celtic Monasticism for Everyday People.* Buxhall: Kevin Mayhew.

Westerhoff, J. (2012) *Will Our Children Have Faith?* (3rd edn). New York: Morehouse Publishing.

Wright, N.T. (2014) *The Way of the Lord: Christian Pilgrimage Today.* Grand Rapids, MI: Eerdmans.

Chapter 9

FAVOURITE TEACHER

Learning the Tenets of Our Faith

Howard Worsley

Introduction

- Is faith taught or caught?

- Is the success of the Gospel as it travels to all parts of the world the sole responsibility of the Church (or of individual Christians), *or* is it God's responsibility?

Our answers to these questions are critical to how we teach the Christian faith to children. In this chapter I reflect on the tension of teaching the faith with the responsibility that it is all down to the teacher and yet with the confidence that it is all down to God. This is the tension between relying on the natural grain of life (connatural experiential learning) and relying on the taught insights of Church historical revelation (systemic doctrinal teaching). Both teaching approaches need to be used. This might be called a balanced pedagogy.

A balanced pedagogy

Way back at primary school my favourite teacher was Mrs Jones. She was an expert at teaching an idea and then letting us children develop the content of that idea by using our imaginations. Half a century later (I am now in my 50s), I can still recall the term we spent learning about the Vikings. Mrs Jones told our class a little bit about Denmark and then about how the ancient Vikings built boats. After this she allowed our imaginations to take over. We were encouraged to build a huge Viking warship in the classroom. We all designed our own individual shields and placed them on the edge of the boat where we sat. This had a huge impact on my imagination and encouraged me to find out more about boats and Viking raiders and of earlier more primitive living conditions.

Ever since then I have had a healthy respect for history. I then went on to learn how to sail, and I now own a small sailing boat. Often as I set out to sea, I imagine the ancient Vikings setting sail into the unknown. I have also now become a habitual researcher, and trace back my first piece of research as being about Vikings. Looking back I consider that Mrs Jones operated a balanced pedagogy, beginning with systemic teaching (using 'rational logic') to introduce us to Viking culture, which she then rapidly allowed the class to unpack (using what we might call 'connatural experience').

Transferring these two pedagogies into how we teach faith to children identifies that there are two processes at work. One is to pass on to children what is known from our faith tradition. This is direct teaching of our particular religious truth that we have come to hold. The other is to draw out the natural insights that a child already has as they process spiritual reality. In other words, we have two models, one that sees itself to be 'putting in' (like the image of filling up an empty vessel) and the other that sees itself as 'drawing out' (like the image of discovering a hidden treasure). The systemic teacher of doctrine might tend to view the child as an empty vessel that needs topping up with knowledge, whereas the experiential teacher might tend to view the child as containing original insights that are buried deep and that need to be unearthed.

A balanced pedagogy will use both the method of 'putting in' (content or curriculum) and of 'drawing out' (process). The method of 'putting in' might be termed 'systemic teaching', whereas the method of 'drawing out' might be termed 'experiential teaching'.

Educationalists who rely on the wisdom of the faith tradition will be more predisposed to systemic teaching. Educationalists who rely on a child's natural inclination will be more predisposed to experiential learning. As anyone who has taught children will have experienced, teaching is a combination of both putting in and drawing out. It involves both the addition of curricular content and the processing of that material.

Similarly one might say that educationalists who rely on the accuracy of the faith tradition that they know will be more predisposed to cataphatic knowledge, while educationalists who are less confident in the accuracy of their faith perceptions are more likely to be more open to a child's natural inclination to have an original vision, and will be more predisposed to apophatic knowledge. Cataphatic knowledge focuses more on the revelation of the faith tradition, drawing on the Scriptures and the creeds, whereas apophatic knowledge is more content to allow the domain of mystery to be present in truth and to acknowledge the limitations of language and of comprehension. Systemic teachers are thereby more likely to want to draw on cataphatic teaching systems, whereas the teachers using experiential learning methods are more likely to draw on a belief that knowledge of the divine is merely apophatic. In the Christian tradition of education, both cataphatic and apophatic epistemologies are present. However, the more conservative traditions of faith will draw towards a cataphatic epistemology and will want to define it in order to pass it on to children. This is certainly true of the more reformed schools of Christian theology and in mainstream Islamic schools. Conversely, the more liberal traditions of faith will champion an apophatic epistemology and will want to allow their children to make their own judgements. This is seen in Quaker meeting halls or in Sufi schools of Islam.

How the Christian faith has been handed down through the centuries

That the faith should be passed on down the generations is taken as read within the Judaeo-Christian traditions and indeed in all the Abrahamic faiths. Writing 1000 years before Christ, the Psalmist spoke of the story of faith being passed down from long before his birth to many generations after his death:

> We will not hide them from their descendants;
> We will tell the next generation
> the praiseworthy deeds of the Lord,
> his power, and the wonders he has done.
> He decreed statues for Jacob
> and established the law in Israel,
> which he commanded our ancestors
> to teach their children,
> so the next generation would know them,
> Even the children yet to be born,
> And they in turn would tell their children. (Psalm 78.4–6)

However, the Psalmist did not say *how* the stories of faith would be passed on down the generations, although a clue is given in the reference to teaching the received law of Jacob. History reveals to us that the Israelite law was passed on principally by religious rituals in annual seasonal festivals (e.g. the Passover), by regular religious devotion through sacrifice, through telling the story in the home and through living lives that were honouring to God. Little is known about the origins of the early Israelite religious world of schooling, and it is disputed as to whether organised schooling existed in the home or in the synagogue. It is not even known with any certainty whether the ancient Jews established schools for their children. As a result, the Hebrew Bible cannot be used to justify an original model of schooling, but it can be used to offer theological insights into the process of education. We can presume that early Israelite children in Old Testament times were taught the faith formally and informally. We might presume that they were taught with the balance of both systemic teaching and experiential learning.

If we are to look at the insights of an ancient educationalist, who was to teach two millennia after the Psalms were written, Thomas Aquinas considered that there were two different ways to attain correct judgement, one using 'perfect use of reason' and the other using 'connaturality'. In more contemporary terms this is an appeal to intellectual judgement (reason) and an appeal to knowledge through inclination (connaturality).

So what does the wider theological tradition teach us about these two pedagogies used in passing on the faith?

Theological reflection on balancing the two pedagogies

The degree to which a Christian teacher will use either systemic or experiential teaching will be determined by their doctrinal stance as well as by temperamental preference. If the teacher believes that the child is in danger of eternal damnation because of their Original Sin, that teacher will be very keen to systemically teach the doctrine of salvation. Conversely, if that teacher believes that the child is in a state of Original Grace, they will want to unearth the blessings of their fresh vision. Of course, this is a simplistic overview of a complex subject, but it is an introduction that allows us to explore it in broad terms as we examine the educational theory. It comes down to whether the teacher believes in Original Blessing or Original Sin.

Looking at theology from a wide-angle lens, Christians tend to put their focus either on *creation or redemption*, *creation* being the very beginning of God's action in making this beautiful and hurting world (including us), *redemption* being the cross-shaped intervention of Jesus in sorting out a broken world. Theologians who focus on creation will talk about Original Blessing, because their emphasis is on God making us in such a way that we are naturally in relationship with him. Their focus is on a time before The Fall, before sin and brokenness. Their vision is attractively positive and they look out on the world seeing God's natural hand on people, whether they know it or not, and as such they expect people (including children) to come to faith in Jesus as a means of *becoming whole*, of completing an initial blessing which comes to fruition. As Blaise Pascal (1623–1662) said, 'The infinite abyss (*of incompletion caused by separation from God*) can be filled only with an infinite and unchangeable object; in other words, by God himself' (Pascal 1999, 10.148; emphasis added).

This line of thought is strongly present in some Roman Catholic theologians, notably Karl Rahner (1904–1984), whose denial of Original Sin (1950) gave birth to the idea of the Supernatural Existential that every person enjoys the fullness of grace and is determined by that grace even when we reject it in sin or guilt (see Worsley 2014). It was also popularised by Matthew Fox in his influential book entitled *Original Blessing* (1983).

Christians who think like this and who work with children may emphasise Nurture above Conversion, and will use the image of a *Seed*. They see the role of the children's worker as watering the *Seed* that is naturally present in the child. They are like a gardener tending seedlings that have been placed by God into the greenhouse of the world.

By contrast is the more traditional teaching of Original Sin that has long been taught as a staple (and previously unchallenged) doctrine by the Catholic and Protestant Churches. It tends to be particularly triumphed by Reformed Churches. Theologians who focus on redemption will talk about Original Sin as a teaching that presumes The Fall from grace (when Adam and Eve were expelled from the Garden of Eden). It will cite the tendency of all humans to deviate from following God naturally, and will emphasise the inherent sinfulness of children and of adults. As the Psalmist says, 'I was born a sinner – yes, from the moment my mother conceived me' (Psalm 51.5). Even if we want to do what is correct, we end up falling short of our best intentions. Such teaching is traced back to Augustine (354–430), whose teaching of Original Sin was popular among the Protestant Reformers Martin Luther (1483–1546) and John Calvin (1509–1564), who equated Original Sin with concupiscence (the innate tendency to sin), affirming that it persisted even after baptism, completely destroying freedom.

Christians who think like this and who work with children may emphasise Conversion above Nurture and will use the image of a *Knot*. They see the role of the children's worker as to undo the *Knot* naturally present in the child. They are like a gardener weeding the soil around the seeds, eradicating weeds from the seeds. Looking back now, I reflect on whether my focus is on Original Blessing or on Original Sin.

Comparative approaches

Adults working with children might see themselves as planting seeds or undoing *Knots* of Original Sin. Experiential teachers might see themselves as tending the seed that was originally planted at birth. Both the image of the seed and the image of the *Knot* carry aspects of educational practice that are both necessary in that it is important that those who communicate the Gospel to children are both nurturers (tenders of the *Seed*) and evangelists (undoers of the *Knot*) (Worsley 2008b). However, the degree to which the children's minister emphasises their theological predisposition will impact the experience of the child.

Those communicating the faith story with children need to work with children who are culturally predisposed to faith as well as those for whom it is alien. It is unhelpful to view children from Christian homes as being 'seeded' and children from non-Christian homes as 'knotted'. Both the images of the *Knot* and the *Seed* can be considered to be biblical, but they carry different emphases in how we tell the faith to children. If children's ministry is viewed from the angle of Original Blessing (using the image of a *Seed*), the child's development will be seen as a gradual dawning, as a child acquires a new awareness of God. As the teacher draws out the child's experiential insights, there is a steady process of understanding that the child is a child of God, much like Timothy, the third generation Christian (2 Timothy 1.5), who inherited the faith from his mother and grandmother. It is like the flowering of a snowdrop that has lain in the frozen ground that appears after winter. Once it was not there, but then it shows itself.

If Children's ministry is viewed from the angle of Original Sin (using the image of a *Knot*), a child's development is seen as being when 'the penny drops'. As the teacher imparts systemic doctrinal insight, the child's former way of thinking is confronted and rejected. From now on it will be different. It might be a one-off moment, like Saul on the road to Damascus (Acts 9.5). Once he was on a road from God, and now he has changed direction and is travelling into God. His teaching was that the old had gone and the new had come (2 Corinthians 5.17) – once he was in the darkness, now he was in the light (Colossian 1.13). To summarise the two approaches offered by emphasising 'Original Sin' (*Knot*) or 'Original Blessing' (*Seed*) within comparative educational methodologies I have created the table below. Connatural experiential learning (relying on the taught insights of Church) is compared with systemic doctrinal teaching (historical revelation).

TABLE 9.1: COMPARISON BETWEEN CONNATURAL
LEARNING AND SYSTEMIC TEACHING

Connatural experiential learning	Systemic doctrinal teaching
Teaching as: Drawing out	Teaching as: Putting in
Teaching as: Processing content/discovery	Teaching as: Adding content/following curriculum
Preference for: Apophatic epistemology	Preference for: Cataphatic epistemology
Knowledge acquired through: Inclination	Knowledge acquired through: Reason
Theology derived from: Original Blessing	Theology derived from: Original Sin
Dominant theological image of: The *Seed*	Dominant theological image of: The *Knot*

Much reflection has been given to the question as to whether it is beneficial or harmful for children's ministry to move away from systemic doctrinal teaching to the more connatural experiential style of learning. Michael Anthony (2006) describes this as a move from 'the Instructional–Analytical Model to the Contemplative–Reflective model'. He is of the opinion that the Contemplative–Reflective approaches often regard the more Instructional–Analytical model as power abuse (Westerhoff 1976), and thereby as being unnecessary due to a child being a thin place where the presence of the divine can break through (Nye 2009).

These approaches raise questions of epistemology concerning how the child knows God or the extent to which the image of God in the child is marred by sin. Does the teacher need to impart the good news of God, or is it something that the children need to discover for themselves? This has further implications for one's understanding of revelation, Scripture and the Spirit as well as of sin in children. What does it look like for a child to genuinely engage with God? Does the contemplative–reflective approach give children the content of the Christian faith that they need to genuinely engage with God? Does the instructional–analytical approach impose a dogma onto children that does not allow them to reflect on the meaning of the story or to play with faith constructs? Will an encounter with God be a sudden conversion or a gradual dawning in the child? From God's perspective, the key thing is that they know His presence, walk with Him and follow His leading. From a child's perspective, the experience of getting to know God might be quite varied.

Therefore, those who teach the faith to children and who are doing so experientially and connaturally, working from the theology of Original Blessing, can be encouraged to relax into God's sovereign purposes and to see themselves as working within the grain of a bigger picture. It does not all depend on them, but on God. Their task is simply to find out what God is doing and to join in. Gone is the anxiety of being overly concerned about eternal destiny. That is a knowledge known only by God, not the minister. However, the flipside to such theology might be an overly laid-back approach that expresses no urgency and becomes disinterested in conversion. Indeed, critics might suggest that such a positive view of the developing child is merely naïve.

From the child's point of view, the experience of being ministered to by someone who believes in Original Blessing is likely to be affirming. They are unlikely to feel coerced or pressurised into making a commitment, merely loved and nurtured in their growth in faith. Critics, however, might suggest that with this model, children might never even be asked to make a response to God at all, because the teacher leaves all impetus with the child.

From the alternative discourse of Original Sin, the image of the *Knot* is more salutary. It is the dominant ideology in Christian doctrinal thought and can be traced back via Paul's discussion of sin in the letter to the Romans in which he is clear that, 'All have sinned and fall short of the glory of God, and all are justified freely by his grace through the redemption that came by Christ Jesus' (Romans 3.23–24). This sinfulness is a taint on all humans as derived through the human ancestry of Adam (Romans 5.12–21). Therefore, those who teach children in a systemic doctrinal manner, working from the concept of Original Sin, will tend to be attentive to the plight of the children they are addressing. The Gospel of salvation has been entrusted to them and they will be mindful that, 'Woe to me if I do not preach the gospel!' (1 Corinthians 9.16). Their emphasis is likely to be more on the responsibility of the teacher than on the sovereignty of God. It is quite likely that there will be a sense of urgency in their need to 'preach the gospel to all creation' (Mark 16.15) and to 'look forward to the day of God and speed its coming' (2 Peter 3.12).

We need to be deeply committed that those who pass on the faith to children, whether systemically or experientially, are not tainted by any form of religious abuse that can arise from unprocessed theology or undeveloped thinking. A good children's teacher will have considered their own theological assumptions and will also be aware that they themselves are becoming 'like little children' (Matthew 18.3).

My favourite teacher puts it into practice

So how are we to teach children in a way that works with a child's experience while also adding the insights of our faith tradition? Personally, I work with a strong sense that if my favourite teacher Mrs Jones was to have taught the Christian faith in church as a children's church teacher (as opposed to working in my childhood primary school), she would have been superb. She would have had a strong sense of the *missio Dei*, a sense that God has been at work in the world long before she arrived, and one that suggested that her task was simply to find out what God was doing and to join in. Applied to passing on the faith to children, it would mean that she would expect to hear spiritual insights of God from the children she was teaching. It would mean that she would respect the children as being emergent theologians who are processing thoughts of God. If she was to offer the systemic doctrine of the Christian faith, it would have been done with humility and offered when the child was ready to hear it. Most of the time, though, she would have been working experientially with children, endeavouring to sense where God was already at work, and she would be working with the flow of that process. To discuss this further, Mrs Jones would initially have had a conversation with the child as she told the story of faith (a). She would then listen to the child (b), reflect with the child (c), and play with the child (d).

a) Telling the story to the child (treating the child as a student)

I know many Sunday School teachers and children's church leaders who speak to children with a balanced pedagogy. They teach just like my favourite teacher Mrs Jones, and they know that the Christian story needs to be told. I refer to them in my book, *A Child Sees God* (Worsley 2009), in which I conclude by offering six rules for telling Bible stories with children in the home, the Church or the school. The six rules are all based on making storytelling an occasion, a key moment in the day when the child is ready to engage:

1. regularity of the occasion

2. importance of the occasion

3. timing of the occasion

4. ambiance of the occasion

5. sacredness of the occasion

6. internal engagement of the occasion.

b) Listening to the child (treating the child as a human)

It is a basic right to be listened to and it is a mark of respect. Mrs Jones listened with the intensity of love, expecting to hear what was fresh and original in the child. Teachers like her bring such an attitude to the transmission of faith, because they have a respect for the child's natural inclination to grow towards the light, working with the connatural presence of what is already present. The teacher who works experientially with the child will first listen in order to get a sense of the child's world. When deep listening takes place, the teacher can look out with the eyes of the child and understand their hopes and fears, to see at the same level and understand the imaginative processes.

If the child is to be heard, encountering the sacred texts of the Bible, then a means of interpretation in context needs to be identified. I call this hermeneutic phenomenology (Worsley 2006). Whereas natural sciences tend to look for truth and knowledge through method and through adherence to a set of rules pertaining to a particular method (van Manen 1990), hermeneutic phenomenology looks for truth and knowledge through interpretation of the expressions of human life (Sharkey 2001). It is a tradition that pays attention to how things appear to be in context (phenomena), and is interpretive of them, noting that all phenomena are encountered through the experience of life and are described as human constructs.

In order to interpret any text, the person needs to be aware of their own lens of meaning that they carry to the text. It follows that, if we are to consider how a child might perceive the ancient text of the Bible, by focusing on a story of interest such as the creation narrative, we must first consider the child's world in order to access their sphere of meaning.

c) Reflecting with the child (treating the child as a theologian)

It is at this stage in the chapter that I need to move from Mrs Jones to the late Professor John Hull, who supervised my doctoral work. John showed more respect to children as learners than any other adult teacher I have met, and for this section he replaces Mrs Jones as my favourite teacher. Although he was totally blind, he took many opportunities to tell stories of faith to children and to discuss with them how they processed the reality of faith. With his own children, he told biblical stories using the systematic doctrinal insights of the faith, and would then have processed the stories using his children's connatural experience. This enabled him to be in a position to reflect with the children theologically, and to record the new insights that emerged. Maybe it was because of his blindness that he focused so strongly on the articulated responses of his own children, writing them down and offering subsequent reflection to them. His published accounts of conversations with children move seamlessly from the happenings of the day to theology and on to playful dialogue about life and the universe. His seminal booklet, *God Talk with Young Children* (Hull 1991), gives us a model of how such conversations can ensue. This little book sets out 33 conversations with young children, mostly about God. The conversations are interpreted and suggestions are made about the art of theological conversation with children. These are conversations that could take place in any context at church, home or place where faith is being considered.

Below is an example of how the concept of death is discussed between a parent and a child, drawing on the child's constructs. It exemplifies a type of conversation that could equally take place between a trusted children's minister and a child (Hull 1991, p.11):

Child (aged three-and-a-half years): Was that man's name Mr Bird?

Parent: Yes.

Child: Was he a bird? [*Laughs*]

Parent: Was he like a bird?

Child: No.

Parent: Why not?

Child: Birds have feathers. [*Laughs*]

Parent: And the man didn't have feathers, did he? He had clothes. [*Both laugh*]

Child: And birds have wings.

Parent: Yes.

Child: Birds die.

Parent: So do people.

Child: [*Silence*]

Parent: What does 'die' mean?

Child: You go to be with God.

Parent: Where is God?

Child: Up in the sky.

Parent: But up in the sky there are clouds.

Child: [*Laughs*] No, but I mean when you go up and up and up past the clouds and you go [*speaking in a little high thin voice*] up and up and up and then you come [*whispering*] to a teeny cottage and in that cottage there's God.

John follows up his godly conversation by discussing it and adding his own interpretation. In this instance, discussing the story above, he notes that:

This young child knew perfectly well that there was something odd about the literal location of God in a place in the sky, but could not express that oddity in the form of a structure of sentences, arranged so as to reason from one sentence to the next. In other words, the child could not say 'when I say "sky" I am referring to a symbol for that which stands over against this earth and our lives. I am trying to say that God is transcendent, and that the dead are likewise translated somehow into this other plane of reality'. No, the child cannot say that or think in those terms, but the child laughs at the question about clouds. Why? The child knows that in asking the question the parent has playfully and perhaps deliberately misunderstood. The child responds not by moving from concrete to abstract thinking, but by using concrete pictures in literal ways. Moreover, the child dramatises the situation by speaking in a higher, smaller voice, suggesting that this is something beyond the ordinary plane which is half comical and yet very serious and important, like a shared secret. The child, being a concrete thinker, cannot respond by drawing attention to the abstract features of the word 'up'. He can only deal with the problem by pushing the literal meaning of the word further and further. Hence you have to go up and up and up...the fact that God's cottage is tiny is the child's concrete way of depicting something which is far away. Cottages seen in the distance do appear tiny. God, as it were, is found in a disappearing point of remoteness. Nevertheless, there is a cottage. The child returns to the homely, the familiar. God is (somehow) an actual person in an actual place but this is not a place like our ordinary places, and his person is not like other people. There are abstract aspects of the word 'up', but the child deals with these in a concrete way. He simply repeats the word again and again. (Hull 1991, p.12)

d) Playing with the child (treating the child as a child)

My favourite teachers, both Mrs Jones and John Hull, were most at home in the company of children. They did not do so primarily out of duty or out of conviction, but out of love. They enjoyed being with them and this was communicated in their playfulness. It is in playing that a reward is returned to the adult because the child reminds us how much fun there is in reflecting on a story and how enjoyable is the process of learning. Both Mrs Jones and Professor Hull were serious educators, but they knew how to play. I cannot help but reflect that my least favourite teachers are just too serious; they cannot play with the story that they are telling because they see it as a rigid revelation that is not open to interpretation. Indeed, I fear that my worst teachers are those who cannot engage with poetry or in symbol in the imagination of faith transmission. What they do is to impose a formality onto the occasion that forces a form of literal interpretation onto the story, forbidding any private interpretation, and thereby trapping the child.

Returning to the playfulness of my favourite teachers, their methodologies for storytelling resonate hugely with the Godly Play method patented by Dr Jerome Berryman. This ordained American educationalist spent close to 40 years creating the methodology of *Godly Play* (Berryman 1995), which is constructed by an experiential pedagogy and supported by an open theology. This approach has been developed in the US by Csinos and Beckwith (2012) and in the UK by Rebecca Nye (2009). Both Mrs Jones and Professor Hull delighted in processing the knowledge that was already present in the child, adding to it at times and encouraging the child to conduct further research at other times. This method of storytelling teaches children the art of using Christian language – parable, sacred story, silence and liturgical action – helping them become more fully aware of the mystery of God's presence in their lives.

Conclusion

My favourite teacher is a mixture of both Mrs Jones with her down-to-earth engagement with children in their own worlds and of Professor John Hull who was someone who delighted in investigating theological assumptions. Aware of the dangers implicit in coercion, these teachers allowed children to access the systematic doctrines of the faith through engaging in connatural experiential learning. They tended to see the telling of the Christian story as the nurturing of a seed that God had already planted, because God has already given the child an Original

Blessing in creation. Through telling the story, listening, reflecting and playing, the story of God is allowed to travel on.

QUESTIONS FOR REFLECTION AND DISCUSSION

- Who was your favourite teacher, and what did you learn from them?

- What or who has been the significant influence on you in relation to your pedagogy?

- How does the dichotomy between Original Sin and Original Blessing impact your approach to children's ministry?

- Which approach do you default to most naturally, connatural experiential learning or systemic doctrinal teaching?

- Does the approach the Church has to learning impact the way you facilitate learning with children, and if so, how?

- In what ways do you tell Bible stories? Are there any insights from this chapter that might impact this for the future?

References and further reading

Anthony, M.J. (ed.) (2006) *Perspectives on Children's Spiritual Formation.* Nashville, TN: B&H.

Berryman, J. (1995) *Godly Play.* Minneapolis, MN: Augsburg.

Csinos, D.M. and Beckwith, I. (2012) *Children's Ministry in the Way of Jesus.* Downers Grove, IL: IVP (Inter-Varsity Press).

Dijkstra, A. and Veenstra, R. (2001) 'Do religious schools matter? Beliefs and life-styles of students in faith-based secondary schools.' *International Journal of Education and Religion 2,* 182–206.

Fox, M. (1983) *Original Blessing.* Rochester, VT: Bear & Company.

Gadamer, H. (1989) *Truth and Method* (2nd rev. English ed., translated by J. Weinsheimer and D. Marshall). London: Sheed & Ward.

Hull, J. (1991) *God Talk with Young Children.* Derby: CEM.

Lipínski, A. (1986) 'Royal and state scribes in Ancient Jerusalem.' *Congress Volume, Jerusalem* (SVT 40), 157–164.

Nye, R. (2009) *Children's Spirituality: What It Is and Why It Matters.* London: Church House Publishing.

Pascal, B. (1999) *Pensées.* London: Penguin.

Parker-Jenkins, M., Hartas, D. and Irving, B. (2004) *In Good Faith: Schools, Religion and Public Funding.* Farnham: Ashgate.

Rahner, K. (1950) 'Eine Antwort.' *Orientierung 14,* 141–145.

Rochberg, F. (2004) *The Heavenly Writing: Divination, Horoscopy and Astronomy in Mesopotamian Culture.* Cambridge: Cambridge University Press.

Sharkey, P. (2001) 'Hermeneutic Phenomenology.' In R. Barnacle (ed.) *Phenomenology, Qualitative Research Methods* (pp.16–37). Melbourne, VIC: RMIT University Press.

Suto, T. (2004) 'Virtue and knowledge: Connatural knowledge according to Thomas Aquinas.' *The Review of Metaphysics,* 61–79.

van Manen, M. (1990) *Researching Lived Experience: Human Science for an Action Sensitive Pedagogy*. London, ON: Althouse Press.

Westerhoff, J.H. III (1976) *Will Our Children Have Faith?* New York: Morehouse.

Westerhoff, J.H. III (2014) 'How to make Christians.' *Children's Work Magazine*, January.

Worsley, H.J. (2006) 'Insights from children's perspectives in interpreting the wisdom of the biblical creation narrative.' *British Journal of Religious Education 28*(3), 249–259.

Worsley, H.J. (2008a) 'Church of England schools as centres of religious abuse or avenues for religious nurture.' *International Journal of Children's Spirituality 13*(1), 75–83.

Worsley, H.J. (2008b) 'Knots, nuts and new sheets (Thinking theologically with educationalists).' *Journal of Anglican Secondary School Headteachers 21*, 24–26.

Worsley, H.J. (2009) *A Child Sees God: Children Talk about Bible Stories*. London: Jessica Kingsley Publishers.

Worsley, H.J. (2014) 'Conversion: A new paradigm.' *Childrenswork Magazine 1*(14), 22–25.

Chapter 10

FAMILY PICNIC

Intergenerational Working

Sam Richards

Jesus loved family picnics! He spent much of his time eating and drinking with others in intergenerational settings. Famously he hosts a couple of enormous picnics (the feeding of the 5000 recounted in all four Gospels and the feeding of the 4000 in Matthew and Mark – we are told the number doesn't include the women and children present!) – giving thanks to God and sharing food. These miracles demonstrate the abundance of God's love and provision, the communal nature of our lives and needs, and how Christ meets all ages in the midst of such sharing. Indeed, 'The best way to be formed in Christ is to sit among the elders, listen to their stories, break bread with them, and drink from the same cup, observing how these earlier generations of saints ran the race, fought the fight, and survived in grace' (Frazier, quoted in Allen and Ross 2012, p.270).

Most of us have happy memories of family picnics – the combination of different generations, sharing food and alfresco settings with space for play, storytelling and conversation can be the stuff of idyllic, inclusive celebrations. Wouldn't it be wonderful if Church was like that…?

Intergenerational

Lois is my biblical hero (2 Timothy 1.5). She is mentioned in passing as Timothy's grandmother, along with her daughter Eunice, Timothy's mother – the first example of intergenerational Christian ministry, passing on a living faith to a young man who would become a Christian leader. Of course, Paul was also part of this intergenerational community, along with many others. In fact, intergenerational was the norm in biblical times because society was based around the family (work, social life, faith, financial and other support), and family meant multiple generations and multiple connections, not the nuclear or fractured family units we default to today. Everyone was part of a family – it did not depend on your age or marital status, your usefulness or future potential:

A father to the fatherless, a defender of widows, is God in his holy dwelling. God sets the lonely in families. (Psalm 68.5–6)

God established human community to be an intergenerational family and makes his promises 'from generation to generation'.

Today's Church should have many different generations within it – infants, children, young people, emerging adults, young adults, middle-aged adults, older adults – as many as seven generations potentially spanning more than ten decades. In fact, the Church is one of the few places in society that remains multigenerational. We are segregated in most of life (home, work, social life), most of the time into groups of predominately one or two generations. But there is a fundamental difference between multigenerational and intergenerational. Churches can cater for these generations separately (with programmes, services and activities aimed at different groups) and be multigenerational. Or churches can cater for these generations together, intentionally creating communities that bring people of all ages together in worship, discipleship, service, mission and ministry: intergenerational. The shift from multigenerational to intergenerational is so counter-cultural, profoundly biblical and vital for the regeneration of the Church, we must engage with this seriously for *all* our sakes.

According to situative–sociocultural theory people learn the ways of a community of practice as they participate authentically and relationally with more experienced members of the culture (Allen and Ross 2012). Research findings from Sticky Faith (Powell and Clark 2011) point to exactly the same conclusion in our churches. A key difference between those children and young people growing up within the Church who stuck with their faith into adulthood and those who didn't (almost half) was the presence of meaningful relationships with Christians beyond their family of different generations. Young people who helped out with younger children, those children and young people who experienced all-age worship, those who had friendships with adults that extended beyond Sunday service attendance, those who had engaged in mission and service alongside other ages rather than just their peer group, they were all more likely to grow up to become Christian adults.

I am not suggesting we ditch children's work! Just that we realise it has a place within a much richer, all-age church family life. 'As a church community we must learn to do only those things in separate age groups which we cannot in all conscience do together' (URC Charter for Children in the Church). To enable enduring faith to develop we need intergenerational contexts and relationships. Otherwise we only have an idea of how to be a Christian at our stage of life and faith. We know we lose people at the points of transition from one generational setting to another: children's work to youth work, youth work to student work, student work to adult church. Part of the problem is the lack of real relationship between the generations – so moving 'up' means starting again with no prior understanding of what it might mean to be a 12-/18-/25-/45-/65-year-old Christian, and how that generational group might relate together. The only role models available are the children and youth workers – no wonder so many young adults who do stick with church seem to believe they need to become church workers to go on with their faith; they have no real knowledge of other ways of living out a deepening discipleship.

If we read Paul's wonderful description of the Church as a body in 1 Corinthians 12, and consider the different parts to be different generations, then we get an incredible sense of how much we need each other if we are to truly be the body of Christ on earth. All are members, not potential members or ex-members. If we allow any generation to feel excluded, or that they do not need those at different ages and stages of faith to themselves, we will be a seriously maimed and deformed body:

> But God has put the body together giving greater honor to the parts that lacked it, so that there should be no division in the body, but that its parts should have equal concern for each other. If one part suffers, every part suffers with it; if one part is honored, every part rejoices with it. Now you are the body of Christ, and each one of you is a part of it. (1 Corinthians 12.24–27)

It is fair to say that the youngest generations are often those that lack honour or respect in our society, and in our churches. Jesus himself challenged this when his disciples turned away children from being blessed (Matthew 19.13–15; Mark 10.13–16). The body picture reminds us how much adults of all ages need children and young people, as well as the other way around. In terms of intergenerational whole-life discipleship, the learning needs to be mutual and two-way. Jesus reminded his disciples of their need to learn from children and their need to learn how to be like children (Matthew 18.1–7; see Richards 2013, Chapter 5). Intergenerational discipleship enables children to share their insights, trust and innate ability to play. Scripture Union has developed *Explore Together* as a resource to enable such intergenerational learning, replacing the sermon slot with open-ended questions to enable all ages to explore and respond to the Bible reading (through a variety of learning zones: seeing, hearing, thinking aloud, reading, doing, reflecting) and then share that learning through feedback that encourages genuine respectful mutuality. A recent Pentecost session I was part of concluded with a child reading a poem on the Holy Spirit they had just written; adults and children giving a guided tour of the city filled with love they had built together with blocks; children complimenting adults on their oil pastel pictures of the Spirit moving; and everyone identifying their contributions to the communal collage. We broadened each other's understanding of the coming of Spirit on the Church, and gave each other space to encounter the Spirit in our own way. This was a truly enriching experience.

This should not surprise us – if we return to the feeding of the 5000, Jesus enabled a child to contribute (bread and fish), blessed this, encouraged adults to facilitate sharing (getting the disciples to organise the people into groups), and ensured that nothing was wasted (gathering up baskets of leftovers). This is a wonderful template for our own attempts at intergenerational discipleship.

Eating and drinking

Of course, no picnic would be complete without food! And food seems to have been at the centre of Jesus' ministry, so much so that his detractors accuse him of being 'a glutton and a drunkard, a friend of tax collectors and sinners' (Matthew 11.19). Tim Chester (2011) argues his excess of food and excess of grace are linked. The Son of Man came 'to seek and to save the lost' (Luke 19.10) – statement of purpose; and this was done by 'eating and drinking' (Luke 7.34) – statement of method. In much of the Gospels Jesus is either going to, at, or coming from a meal! He told stories about meals to help us understand his Kingdom. Meals were also central to the life of the early Church in Acts. The Passover and the Last Supper, both instituted as meals of remembrance, also illuminate that we are rescued and saved for a meal in the presence of God.

Meals create community – they happen in a place of hospitality, a welcoming, caring space where people are provided for both physically (with food and drink) and socially (with attention and relationship). Shared meals, and picnics in particular, can cater for all tastes and needs while enabling communal feasting. When everyone brings something to share, everyone receives the food as the gift it is, and there is opportunity to try new things and broaden our tastes. Everyone's contribution is welcomed.

Food is a central ingredient in our experience of God's goodness – and it is delicious, not just nutritious! Eating is also an expression of our dependence on God and each other – food forces us to live in community, to share, to cooperate and to trade (Chester 2011). In most cultures, major events in personal, family or community life are celebrated with a meal – think of birthdays, weddings, Thanksgiving, Christmas!

Jesus is seen as both the guest at many meals and host of some. He often emphasises the need to welcome everyone to the table and to treat everyone equally at the table. In Jewish culture, 'with whom am I allowed to eat?' was an important question, as the food laws that helped create their identity also set up 'purity' barriers between people. Jesus eats with all the wrong people and makes this irrelevant – emphasising everyone's equal need and equal access to grace. Similarly, in intergenerational church we need to move away from the need to make everyone 'behave properly' and rediscover an emphasis on belonging. We shouldn't expect the different generations to have the same ideas about appropriate clothing, noise levels, use of mobile phones and so on. So we need to find ways of enabling understanding and respect through relationship rather than policing. After all, at a picnic no one should be told off for eating with their fingers rather than 'correctly' using their cutlery, however old they are! At a picnic there is the freedom to enjoy different things together, to move between spectating, engaging, serving and being served – a fluidity of roles and relationships among the generations.

Eating together establishes our shared status as guests at the Lamb's table or picnic blanket, each bringing our offering to share together and enrich our shared experience. When we separate in church to spend time in a peer age group, doing the activities we prefer (such as listening to a sermon, craft and games, Bible study, drama or service project planning), we can ensure that we come back together and enable each group to share what they have been doing to enrich the life of the whole church. I love it when our local vicar invites the couple of children who have been colouring and sticking at the back of the church to come and show everyone their creations – valuing how they have spent time with God while others have been praying the liturgy. I also love it when children are invited to ask the adults what they have been doing, and hearing adults consolidate their learning as they put it into words for little ones. It feels like children showing the treasures they have found (feathers, shells, stones, leaves) and adults sharing conversations they've been having ('we've just been talking about …') at a family picnic!

Al fresco

Picnics traditionally take place out of doors, like BBQs and campfires. The fresh air offers shared risk of inclement weather, and a lack of clear boundaries to the space – a church without walls. This allows everyone to choose their place relative to everyone else, with the freedom to sit on a chair, sit on the ground, or run around, as they feel the need. The informal setting allows everyone to shift between participation and spectating, whole group and subgroup activity and attention, with a natural flow. At a picnic some very young and older people might even drop off to sleep for a time!

Being outside offers the opportunity to connect with nature. There is an overwhelming amount of research emphasising how important time spent in the open air is for mental health, physical health and spiritual wellbeing. Time spent outside with others fosters strong relationships through shared experience. It also fosters a sense of connection to the natural world as a living thing, generating awe and wonder. Experts are now starting to talk about a 'nature connection deficit', particularly among children and young people, as the time they spend freely roaming and playing outside has drastically reduced in recent times (Layard and Dunn 2009). Of course, they now roam the virtual world of the internet from the 'safety' of their homes instead.

The natural world is, of course, God's creation, and offers us another 'text' to read that does not require literacy skills. As we engage with and explore nature, we discover more about our Creator, and our relationship with him. We are moved to worship, through wonder at the sheer beauty and intricacy of a tree, leaf or acorn. We are honoured by the momentary presence of a squirrel or bird we observe that notices us, and ushered into the presence of God through that relationship with otherness. We are awed by the size of the ocean, mountain or night sky, and aware of our tiny yet loved place in God's magnificent universe:

When I consider your heavens,
the work of your fingers,
the moon and the stars,
which you have set in place,
what is mankind that you are mindful of them,
human beings that you care for them? (Psalm 8.3–4)

These are experiences open to and common to all ages – even more importantly, ones we can share together in intergenerational contexts.

Children will notice very different things to adults on the same walk or beach. So we need to create opportunities to enjoy God's creation together as an important element of intergenerational whole-life discipleship. Nature walks, open-air services, litter clearing in the park, kite flying, den building, sponsored cycle rides, church camping weekends – there are numerous ways we can build this into our family life and our church family life. Some churches have now taken on allotments as a way of engaging with the local community – a fantastic opportunity for all-age activity, sharing expertise and enthusiasm, learning how to grow food and tend the earth together. Why not hold the Harvest Festival there as a community all-age event with al fresco food to celebrate God's faithful provision?

The 'without walls' dimension of a picnic also helps dissolve the boundary between the Church gathered and the Church sent, between Sunday services and the rest of the week. A picnic takes place in a public space, common land, neutral ground, with the rest of life carrying on around it. People walking by might see someone they know and join in. Family members might arrive late or leave early to enable participation in some other area of life. The world comes into the Church, and the Church is in the world in a more tangible way. We need to expand our thinking about intergenerational church to include life beyond church gatherings, and encourage and resource intergenerational whole-life discipleship to permeate more widely. We need to enable families to worship together at home. We need to envisage church service projects (food banks, hospital visiting, giving, two-thirds of world development projects) as all-age activities and intentionally involve children and young people alongside other ages. We need to design missional endeavours that can include everyone (living nativity, Palm Sunday procession, Messy Church, all-age Alpha). And we need to ensure that when we gather together as a church we are enabling all to play a role and contribute to our worship (welcome, prayer, reading, teaching, singing, testimony, giving). This is how we enable children to grow up and find their place within the family of God – by giving them a place from the start.

Space for play and storytelling

I am blessed to be part of a 'fresh expressions' community that does church along the lines of a family picnic. We are fairly small, and our gatherings are chaotic at times, but we are finding ways of growing in faith together. We meet in local parks or borrowed venues with large lounge or garden areas. We spread out the picnic blankets and share food and fun, worship and fellowship. We (all generations) take turns to cuddle the babies, lead the singing, play with the children (who outnumber the adults), facilitate the prayers, pass round the biscuits, read the Bible, catch up with each other's lives, provoke creativity, share stories, enable conversation and learning. I remember when my daughter, aged five, in the midst of fraught discussions about future changes, drew a very large heart on a piece of paper and asked each of us to write what we loved about our church community in that heart – a simple process to facilitate us remembering what we held dear as we sought to find shared solutions.

One of my favourite gatherings involved the children teaching us all some games. One four-year-old got us all playing 'scary dinosaurs', which basically involved roaring and chasing each other – and lots of laughter!! A glorious game with no point, no means of winning, no rules – but enormous fun and very bonding. 'And a little child shall lead them' (Isaiah 11.6) promises Isaiah as he foretells the coming of Jesus, 'a shoot will come up from the stump of Jesse' (Isaiah 11.1). And children will lead us into the presence of God in very different ways to adults if we give them the opportunity, through their different view of the world (where a wolf can live peaceably with a lamb), through their gifts of play and trust (the passage goes on to talk about the young child putting its hand into a viper's nest unharmed!).

When families share a meal, they also tend to share stories. My extended in-laws always recount infamous family adventures (particularly ones that make fun of my husband!) over Sunday lunch, and the audience now includes our daughter. Memories are passed on, and stories bind us together. Good intergenerational gatherings often produce instances that become the stories shared next time we meet. My church community tells the story of the misty winter's morning when a horse's head suddenly appeared in the circle of people sharing bread and wine (attracted by the smell of food, we presume) – scaring some and delighting others! It has become a parable for us about how we respond to the stranger (who might be an angel in heavy disguise). For stories enable meaning-making and are the most intergenerationally accessible media for this. Shared stories also give us shared reference points and language. The death of a very close family member was made easier to process for my young daughter by our shared three-generational family love of the Narnia books. Being able to talk about someone we loved going to Aslan's country was much more accessible and real than a rather vague idea of 'heaven'.

We all love a good story. I remember Walter Wangerin at the Greenbelt Festival holding an audience of 500 one- to ninety-one-year-olds in the palm of his hand as he told us stories. Children like to ask questions that provoke stories as answers. Children enjoy playing with stories when invited to 'wonder' about them (as the excellent Godly Play approach encourages with Bible stories). The Passover meal puts children in the position of asking the questions to provoke the telling of the story – this is something we could seek to emulate in our churches and families. We also need to tell and retell the story of who we are as a community, and enable the children to contribute, building our sense of identity as the family of God. This is how we tell ourselves into the great salvation story – interweaving our stories as the people of God stories with the Bible stories of the same.

The heavenly banquet

Allen and Ross (2012, pp.270–271, emphasis added) describe their vision for Church and remind us of the conditions necessary to enable this to be:

> People of all ages and maturity levels are present, actively carrying on the very essentials of Christianity… All benefit from each other with a sense of mutuality; in essence they grow each other up into Christ. But for intergenerational Christian formation to happen, the generations must *be* together; they must *know each other*; and they must experience life in the body of Christ *together*.

The image of an intergenerational family picnic gives us some clues as to how we might realise this:

> Blessed is the one who will eat at the feast in the kingdom of God. (Luke 14.15)

Jesus presents Heaven as a great banquet – the biggest intergenerational family picnic ever to which every member of God's family is invited. In fact at this picnic we will all be children – our invitation is to come together as children of our heavenly Father. We pray 'your kingdom come, your will be done on earth as it is in heaven', so we are praying for God to transform our church life: 'when you mix together meaningful participation, radical hospitality and intergenerational community, you create a potent catalyst for generating an ecclesial culture for nurturing children's spiritual formation' (Csinos and Beckwith 2013, p.142). Now doesn't that sound like a heavenly family picnic?

QUESTIONS FOR REFLECTION AND DISCUSSION

- Has Church been a place of intergenerational discipleship for you? Who are your spiritual grandparents, aunts, uncles, cousins, nephews and nieces?

- What are your best and worst memories of all-age Church activities?

- How could your church foster more interaction between the generations?

- How could your church enable different ages to share their experiences of God?

- What role does food play in the life of your church?

- How might intergenerational hospitality be encouraged in your church?

- How might your church facilitate nature connection?

- How might playing together become part of your church life?

- How might sharing stories become part of your church life?

- Look at the United Reformed Church's (URC) Charter for Children below. How does this challenge your church's understanding of the place of children in the Church?

CHARTER FOR CHILDREN IN
THE CHURCH: THE TEN POINTS

1. Children are equal partners with adults in the life of the church.

2. The full diet of Christian worship is for children as well as adults.

3. Learning is for the whole church – adults and children.

4. Fellowship is for all – each belonging meaningfully to the rest.

5. Service is for children to give, as well as adults.

6. The call to evangelism comes to all God's people of whatever age.

7. The Holy Spirit speaks powerfully through children as well as adults.

8. The discovery and development of gifts in children and adults is a key function of the church.

9. As a church community we must learn to do only those things in separate age groups that we cannot in all conscience do together.

10. The concept of the 'Priesthood of all Believers' includes children.

Online Resources

Explore Together Resource Books, Green, Blue, Purple, Orange – see scriptureunion.org.uk or exploretogether.org

URC (United Reform Church) Charter for Children in the Church (no date). Available at https://urcshop.co.uk/charter-for-children-pack [Contains a full-colour A4-size version of each of the images by Neil Thorogood with questions for discussion with a Bible reading and a prayer.]

References and further reading

Allen, H. and Ross, C. (2012) *Intergenerational Christian Formation: Bringing the Whole Church Together in Ministry, Community and Worship.* Downers Grove, IL: IVP (Inter-Varsity Press) Academic.

Chester, T. (2011) *A Meal with Jesus: Discovering Grace, Community and Mission around the Table.* Nottingham: IVP (Inter-Varsity Press).

Csinos, D.M. and Beckwith, I. (2013) *Children's Ministry in the Way of Jesus.* Downers Grove, IL: IVP (Inter-Varsity Press).

Herdman, L. and Smith, L.S. (2015) *Explore Together – The Journey.* Bletchley: Scripture Union.

Hilborn, D. and Bird, M. (2003) *God and the Generations: Youth, Age and the Church Today.* Carlisle: Paternoster.

Kirk, D. (2001) *Reconnecting the Generations: Empowering God's People, Young and Old, to Live, Worship and Serve Together.* Buxhall: Kevin Mayhew.

Layard, R. and Dunn, J. (2009) *A Good Childhood: Searching for Values in a Competitive Age.* London: Penguin/The Children's Society.

Mountstephen, P. and Martin K. (2004) *Body Beautiful? Recapturing a Vision for All-age Church.* Cambridge: Grove Books.

Powell, K. and Clark, C. (2011) *Sticky Faith: Everyday Ideas to Build Lasting Faith in Your Kids.* Grand Rapids, MI: Zondervan.

Richards, A. (2013) *Children in the Bible: A Fresh Approach.* London: SPCK.

Roberto, J. (2007) *Best Practices in Intergenerational Faith Formation.* Available at www.faithformationlearningexchange.net/uploads/5/2/4/6/5246709/best_practices_in_intergenerational_faith_formation.pdf

Chapter 11

SUPERHERO, ADVOCATE AND IDOL

Ruth Radley

Introduction

What does the term 'child rights' mean to you? Does it make you bristle? Does it make you excited about the possibilities to both stand up and advocate for our children, and bring them up in a responsible way, thinking of others? Does it concern you within a Christian context? Does it overwhelm you with the responsibility we have as children's advocates, both here and around the world?

Rights in a global nation

Wall (2017) states that in the UK, child poverty stands at a higher rate than the overall poverty rate. Since few adults would be willing to give up their rights – as they provide human dignity, and also as adults broadly speaking have more power and rights than children – it follows that children's rights may need greater consideration. Wall also recognises that simply 'having' a right may not be the same as 'enjoying it in reality' (2017, p.7). However, there has long been concern that to give a person 'rights' is actually a non-biblical concept with much debate. Scott (2007) notes that problems are caused by the idea in some Christian circles that the subject of child rights is secular work and therefore inappropriate in Christian-based work. Both Jesus and Paul demonstrated the laying down of personal rights in the interests of other people (Stephenson 2003), leading some Christians to believe that rights are therefore not compatible with a Christian worldview. Interestingly the earliest version of child rights (heavily inclined as adult responsibility towards children, rather than the individual rights of children) came through a Christian, Eglantyne Jebb, who noted the despicable conditions in which children were living at the conclusion of the Second World War (Collier 2009, p.86). At the heart of rights documents is the understanding that each individual person has dignity that must be protected and for which it must be advocated; Christians believe this dignity comes from being made in the image of God. Indeed, the United Nations Convention on the Rights of the Child (UNCRC) (UN 1989) preamble speaks of the dignity and worth of the human person. For possibly different reasons there is a common understanding of human value and worth that can be utilised.

There are differing thoughts on rights in the Bible. Scott contends that rights as understood today occur but once in the Bible, in the Book of Psalms (140.12), and then only in a few contemporary translations (Scott 2007). However, it has also been suggested that there were rights in the Old Testament. For example, according to Mosaic Law there are distinctions between the people of Israel and foreigners, men and women, slave and free. Although each group had rights, they were not equal (Taber 2002). In the New Testament Jesus taught that all were equal, as did Paul in Galatians 3.28: 'There is neither Jew or Gentile, neither slave nor free, nor is there male and female, for you are all one in Christ Jesus.' Professing Christians therefore need to balance the Old Testament teaching with its development in the New Testament, and when looking at child rights, also take into account the many parts of the Bible where God demands that children are cared for, protected and able to participate.

However, it cannot be denied that the UNCRC does echo Western values, which, by and large, are heavily dependent on a Christian worldview, a rather ironic fact given that some Christians struggle with the concept (Collier 2009). Although many argue that this is Western imperialism (Taber 2002), it is noteworthy that when the UNCRC was brought to be ratified, a large number of non-Western developing countries signed it unreservedly, whereas the UK held reservations on immigration laws and juvenile detention (which were finally lifted in 2008), and the US to date has not signed it at all (Wells 2009). With the emphasis the UNCRC has on the individual child, it could be a fair argument, since many African Nations, for example, work more with a community mindset than an individual one – a child is seen to belong to the whole community, not just the individual parents (Mbiti 1969). Could it not be said that it is also a strong biblical understanding of children too? Griffiths states that the most commonly translated word in the Old Testament for family is *mish-paw-khah*, a word that 'carries within it a sense of Clan or Community' (Griffiths 2017, p.50). This is perhaps something that the Western world needs to re-learn from other nations that still celebrate this family. However, Marshall and Parvis (2004) insist that rights do help to address the consequences of a disjointed society, not generate one.

God's desire that children are protected, nurtured and not harmed can be seen through the pages of Scripture. It would appear that child survival has been a challenge for thousands of years. Jeremiah's Lamentations see the prophet weeping over children and infants dying and fainting in the streets; he implored others to rise in the night and plead for their children (Lamentations 2.19). In Exodus 1.15–21, all midwives were commanded by the King to kill all Hebrew baby boys, though they dared to disobey the King and did not do so, such was their conviction that this was abhorrent to God.

Today, there are many ways in which the survival of children is threatened, in the UK and in the wider world. We hear stories of refugees walking many miles to safety, sometimes parents having to bury family members, including children, along the way – the most vulnerable being affected the worst by famine. In the UK a recent report by the *British Medical Journal* (Mayor 2017) has revealed that there is a widening gap in the health of rich and poor children, with infants from the poorest families having a higher death rate.

All through history, children have been affected by the consequences of the selfish desires of adults, and are often the ones most affected by the evil around us. It is clear from the Bible that God expects children to be protected. It seems to be a narrative through the Bible – 'don't harm my children'. In Exodus 2 we see the mother of the baby Moses, desperate to preserve the life of her child from an evil ruler, hide him in a basket in a river, leaving her elder daughter to watch over him.

Rights and responsibilities

Many international non-governmental organisations (NGOs) working around the world are using child rights as a platform for their work in developing nations. While working in South Sudan, it became apparent during a discussion with the South Sudanese team that we needed to start addressing the subject of child rights in a Christian setting, and encouraging and assisting the church to advocate for their children. However, we became concerned that the rights language that was being used included no reference to the responsibilities a person expecting to have rights should be prepared to exercise. There was considerable concern among adults who had heard radio broadcasts about child rights but who were confused about their own role in this, being unaware that as caregivers, although they still had authority over the children, such authority should be used wisely to encourage the children and not to crush them. On one occasion, my co-worker Samuel visited a community to lead a new training session introducing our work. He asked the participants if they had heard of child rights. Yes, they had all heard, from the radio and seen posters, and so on. He then asked what they felt about them. One prominent pastor stood up and declared, 'We do not agree with them. Before these came, our children were well behaved, now they are spoilt.' However, the pastor continued with the three-day course. On the last day, Samuel conducted an evaluation of the training. The same pastor stood up and declared, 'If this is your understanding of rights, why have you not been to train us before? We can work with this, we want our children to survive, develop and reach their full potential; we want them to have responsibilities.' This pastor had moved from his initial scepticism to become the most supportive member of the community. He even used his own precious fuel to travel around the area on his motorbike, informing the community of further training and other child-related events. It has been interesting to note that when we have explained our work to UK churches we have frequently been told that this training is needed in the UK too, both to help children understand their responsibilities, and adults to understand their role in this.

Concerns about child rights include that there is an agenda to create a universal culture. With understanding, this need not be the case; many articles can be interpreted to fit different cultures. For example, to help a group of student teachers in South Sudan understand the difference between a 'need' (or right) and a 'want' – no mean feat when some tribal languages do not have different words! – they were asked to do an exercise, writing on small pieces of paper all the things they felt children wanted or needed to survive, develop and reach their full potential. The group then together discussed each item and decided if it should go into the 'need' or 'want' pile. A conversation was had over the item 'clothes'. The group decided that this was a need, the whole class agreed, so it was placed in the 'needs' pile. Suddenly Tanabor, one of the students, intervened. 'But, Madam', he said, 'clothes are a want. I studied up to P2 [primary school Year 2] as naked as the day I was born, it did me no harm.' The area Tanabor was from did indeed have nakedness as an acceptable part of the culture. As I stood before the class, I silently reminded myself not to let my culture get in the way of this discussion. 'Okay', I said slowly, 'in my culture, you would die very quickly in the winter if you were not wearing clothes, so for us they are a need.' 'That may be so, Madam', said Tanabor triumphantly, 'but for us it is hot. For us clothes are a want.' After much discussion, we concluded that depending on the local culture clothes could be a need *or* a want, but that where they were a 'want' and not a 'need', caution should be exercised to ensure that there was no hurt or abuse resulting from nakedness.

While doing foundational Bible studies on the four categories of rights, one area of deliberation was the occasions in the Old Testament in which children were expected (and even required) to ask questions (Exodus 12.26; Joshua 4.6). The ensuing discussion with the participants centred on the pros and cons of this. The culture was such that it was seen to be inappropriate for a child to approach an adult to ask questions; they could only speak when the adults approached them. Some parents felt it was time for that culture to change and said that they were comfortable allowing their children to approach with questions at any time. Others said that they felt that was not appropriate at all, and rather disrespectful. Again, with discussion, agreement came that those who felt it was not appropriate would give their children ample opportunities to ask questions; the adult was still making the first move, but doing so regularly, so the children had the opportunity to ask what they needed to ask.

There are implications here for children's workers in the UK. We have many different nations already represented in the UK and continuing refugees and asylum-seekers from other nations joining us – within this there is a countless diversity of cultures. My own experience in South Sudan has taught me that it is not enough to simply 'tell' people about children's rights. There needs to be time for exploration and questioning, allowing space for wrestling with new concepts and time to come to a fresh understanding of the environment in which they find themselves. As churches take the lead in advocating for child rights, it could be that this is an area deserving of further examination as people are assisted to understand the meaning of child rights in a UK culture. It is my strong belief that on the whole, in the UK, the strength of culture is not understood, because ours has changed so much over the last century, and now it is very fluid, with many choices about lots of things. Many cultures in the world have but one way of doing things, and it may not be changed. This needs to be taken into account when working with children and families of different cultures, and grace given, while trying ourselves to learn with open minds, and to see things from a different perspective. We are not always right, of course – the laws of a country are law and need to be adhered to – but I believe that help with understanding these laws is key.

If refugees or asylum-seekers live in your area, seek for ways to befriend and support, ask about their cultures and values, and be aware of things that we do which may affect those in this situation (e.g. bonfire night – it took me a long time when I heard fireworks not to immediately think of gunfire and to listen to see what else was happening outside). Be especially aware when there are children – do we need to campaign for silent fireworks? Or can we prepare people beforehand for the noise they will hear? Are there churches in your area where people are predominantly from a different culture? Do your churches mix? Can you spend time sharing and learning? Are there mosques, temples, synagogues or gurdwaras near you? Has your church family got links with the leaders and congregations? Can you share with each other, striving to understand more about the culture and faith that is being expressed, without an agenda to 'convert'? Is there someone nearby from whom you can learn more about different cultures?

The advocating Church?

According to Marshall and Parvis (2004, pp.185–186):

> We live in a society in which there is in many ways no longer a Christian ethical consensus – or rather in which the Christian values that *have* helped shape our society and continue to influence it are by so many no longer held on consciously Christian grounds... That means that using rights language helps us to communicate. It helps us to take our rightful place, we might say, in public debate. (original emphasis)

The Bible has a lot to say about standing up for the oppressed, for justice, for those who have no voice (Isaiah 1.17). Children often do not have the voice that they need, and sometimes require someone to be that voice for them, speaking out on their behalf. The Church should not be playing catch-up with the so-called 'secular' world in the area of protecting children, belatedly but increasingly allowing them to participate, ensuring that their voices are heard, enabling them to develop as God intended them to. Rather, the Church should be out in the front, fearlessly leading the way in speaking out about children's rights, AND their responsibilities, as well as the responsibilities of their caregivers and the wider community. The Church should be holding the government to account on behalf of our children, as well as actively encouraging them – where appropriate and in relation to their age and stage of development – to be their own advocates by giving them support, opportunities and respect. There is so much potential for the Church to have a real voice in community life if she chooses to, for example, in those areas in which churches organise food banks.

Another way in which the Church has an opportunity to make a difference is in the area of fostering and adoption. According to the organisation Home for Good, if one family in every church in the UK adopted or fostered a child, the care system would be cleared, and each child would have a loving home.[1] Of course, it's not so simple, and there are many challenges along the way, but how often do churches raise this issue, challenging congregations to look into this possibility? Churches are in a perfect place to gather around a family, helping and supporting, practically, financially and prayerfully. Psalms tells us that God puts the lonely into families (Psalm 68.6), yet we have so many children in our care systems feeling alone. Are we willing to act as well as speak out?

We have looked at Scripture in regard to children, and the need for the Church to stand up, have a voice and be counted in the fight for our children. However, the Church is a global family, so is it enough to only have a voice for children in this country? We understand our God is a God of justice, but some of our lifestyle choices in this country are actively funding the oppression of children in other countries. Can we really stand up and be counted speaking out for children here in the UK when our fashion habits, our desire for increasingly better technology and our 'sweet tooth' mean that children (not to mention adults) in other nations are enslaved and trafficked? I am not insinuating that we are to be the 'saviours' of these places and must go to 'make changes'; rather, I suggest that we look at our own lifestyles in our own communities and start to identify where we may need to think about making a difference. Many churches are campaigning for the plight of refugees, offering them homes, petitioning the government to ensure better treatment given, while also initiating all-age outreach programmes to help integration into British society. All these things are good, of course, but as a matter of integrity should we not also consider the fact that our lifestyles are continuing to contribute to some of the wars being faced around the world that affect children? Can we really express horror every time we read of another war story creating refugees, famines and orphans, when we know we sometimes contribute, with our love of mobile phones that use minerals from unofficial production lines, often with child labour, and so contributing to wars (Enough Project[2])? If we are truly talking about holistic children's ministry and being part of a worldwide family, I do not believe we can separate the issues and hold real integrity.

Some things churches can do include:

---

1 See www.homeforgood.org.uk/about-us
2 https://enoughproject.org/about

- Invite a speaker from Home for Good to your church to share.

- Get involved in some of the campaigns around child trafficking, such as Stop the Traffik.[3]

- Look at organisations such as Labour Behind the Label[4] and Ethical Consumer[5] to see which shops are treating overseas workers and the environment fairly, and look for ways to lobby those that aren't, or consider supporting charity shops more in the UK for clothing.

- Begin lobbying phone and computer companies[6] about fuelling war through the elements needed to produce phones.

- The Oxford VIVA Doorsteps[7] campaign discovered that there were real huge needs from children and young people in Oxford. What are the needs in your community? What organisations are present that you can link with? How can the Church, intergenerationally, be involved in meeting those needs?

Superman, Wonder Woman or the Incredible family

A report published by the Church of England, *Rooted in the Church* (2016), concludes that:

- Churches should aim to build a culture of intergenerational relationships.

- Churches should be inclusive of all ages in both leadership and worship.

- Churches should recognise young people and young adults as equal members of the Body of Christ.

- Churches should be encouraged to consider the possibility of admitting baptised children to Communion before Confirmation.

- Churches should become unconditionally welcoming places for young people.

---

3   www.stopthetraffik.org
4   http://labourbehindthelabel.org/our-work/what-brands-should-do
5   www.ethicalconsumer.org
6   See www.ethicalconsumer.org/buyersguides/phonebroadband/mobilephones.aspx
7   http://doorsteps.viva.org

This research began with children aged 11, but I would contend that the results are also applicable to younger children, in relation to their age and stage of development. The title of this section refers to the film, *The Incredibles*. The ending of this film is thought-provoking, because to defeat the Omnidroid it requires the whole Incredible family, including the children, and in addition, Frozone, a family friend, not to mention Edna who designs their supersuits. The wider family, intergenerationally fighting together for the common good, is, to me, a picture of how the Church should be – each using their own gifts and skills for the benefit of others. What a contrast to many of our churches in which there is segregation of different age or experience groups, with no real mixing and sharing together. Children are rarely seen as full and equal members, given a voice into issues that affect them or able to lead. McConnell (2007) argues that children should be seen as part of the laity and ministry teams, and nurtured as they minister to others.

Child's participation is a major component of child rights, recognising the child as a powerful individual. Myers (1999) discusses the merits of community participation leading to their empowerment; this is something that is seen through current work in South Sudan, and other nations, especially through the work of Tearfund,[8] working with communities at their own pace and seeing communities rise up, realising who they are and what resources are available to them. Indeed, when working in the realm of child rights, it is imperative, as well as working with the children, that much work is also undertaken with the adults. Empowering children to have participation in their communities and churches may well have the opposite impact if the adults are not also empowered about these issues.

Hart's (1992) 'The Ladder of Participation' is a well-known tool in this area, and ranges from 'tokenistic, coercive or manipulative', where children are participating but basically doing what they have been told to do by adults, or have been able to have a voice but not with real understanding of the issues, to cooperation with adults, designing, planning and executing things, to a totally child-led approach, with adult supervision as appropriate.

My experiences in South Sudan made me realise that in the past in the UK I had not been as empowering as I might have been to the children in my care in my church. I listened to them, and made them feel important, but they neither led nor had a voice into how weekly sessions or services were planned. They may have been asked to do a prayer or a reading, but they were not able to influence the structure or content. We followed the

---

8   https://learn.tearfund.org/en/themes/church/church_and_community_mobilisation

same themes as the adults, but a team of adult leaders did all the planning. In a weekly small group for the older children, there were possibilities for planning and leading sessions, but, of course, allowing this only in a small group setting no doubt denied us the possibility of learning what the children could teach and share with us on a bigger scale. Consider:

- In your church family, where are the intergenerational activities? If there aren't any, can you work with all ages to plan some?

- Where is the children's voice in areas such as services? Do they get a chance to affect the content? Are they able to contribute more than simply doing a reading? Is there an opportunity for children to preach, for example? To join the music group if that's their gifting? Think of ways in which children's voices can be heard, and how children can actively take a lead in things.

The Ironman factor

As Collier (2009) states, the UNCRC overall values the place of parents guiding their children, something else that is a strong biblical stance. However, some churches have, particularly over the last decade, begun to employ children's pastors whose role is to oversee children's ministry within the church and also to reach out to children not yet in the church. This is often a positive step forward for many churches, especially since we know that 80 per cent of all Christians made their choice as a child (Griffiths 2017). There are, however, some significant weaknesses and dangers attached to this approach.

A potential pitfall for enthusiastic children's workers is that, due to the busy lifestyle of parents, they may inadvertently take on the role of parent, doing for children what God has ordained parents to do. In Exodus 12.21–28 we see the commands for the Passover meal, which happened in the family setting, and served, year-in year-out, as a teaching for children of an alive and active God (Griffiths 2017). Careful attention needs to be given to ensure that parents and caregivers are empowered and resourced to do their work well and not disempowered by the church's children's team (Miles 2003).

Of course, as has been mentioned above, integration with different generations is also crucial, but is often lacking with separate programmes, all ages missing out on much richness and learning with and from each other. We can put so many resources into different areas of ministry yet miss something profound in our separation. Powell (2007) states that children minister through their actions of worship, prayer, questions, advice and stories, and purely through their being. In his book, *Children, Can You Hear Me?*, Brad Jersak shares a story of his young child being present on an evening in which he was speaking to students. As the sung worship was happening, his young child was in his arms. He asked his child what Jesus was saying, and immediately understood the response the child gave as being relevant to the gathering – indeed, many young people responded to the words when they were given out, even though it is quite possible that the child himself didn't understand the word given. Remembering how God worked through the young Samuel in the Bible (Samuel 3), and the difficult message he was given to share with Eli, I find myself frequently wondering how much the Church as a whole misses out on when the children go to their Sunday groups more often than when they are in with the wider church family.

As has been previously mentioned, community is a very important biblical concept – all are needed for different things, and all are valid, the young and old teaching and sharing with each other. When a named person heads up the children's ministry, the danger is that not only does the congregation tend to abrogate its own responsibility for the children, but also that the children's pastor feels that they should lead everything, often not including the children in the planning or delivery. Teaching may become the main emphasis while opportunities to experience the presence of Jesus is neglected, filling the children with head knowledge but not heart experience and the ability to step out in faith.

While I worked in Canterbury as a children's worker in a church, a mother shared with me that she once entered her kitchen in time to hear her daughters finishing a song – complete with dance routine – and heard, 'that's how she does it!' triumphantly from one of the girls. When she enquired what they meant, the reply was, 'that's how Ruth does it at church'. What a realisation for me that I was being mimicked! In many ways this is very flattering, but of course there are dangers. We teach children, and in doing so, use our own interpretation of Scripture, perhaps using what we have been brought up with. Looking back on my ministry over the years, there are things that I would teach differently to children with the life experience that I now have, and further studying that I have done. Of course, this is life – we constantly change as we mature, experience and learn new things ourselves, but we must be careful of what and how we are teaching young minds. Very often in camps and children's sessions, opportunities are given to respond to Jesus, which is often reported in numbers of children who 'became Christians' in that event. However, it may well be that children are responding to something new they have learned about Jesus, 'ongoing conversion experiences' (Griffiths 2009, p.164) rather than 'becoming a Christian', or may even be responding purely to please their leader, or even because of the way the leader has invited the opportunity manipulatively, albeit unconsciously so. Also, when a child holds a leader in such high esteem, what happens when they disappoint? For a child, this can mean their whole world crashing down.

We long for our children to grow up attached to Jesus and not a children's worker, however loving they are or however deep their faith is. There is a real danger of dependency. There is a debate in children's songs as to whether Jesus is a superhero – according to Hillsong Kids he is, but Captain Alan maintains he is not; however you see this, Jesus IS the only one our children need ultimately to be dependent on, not the children's worker! Of course, this does need to be done with caution, but as far as is healthily possible for the children – and leaders – allow them to see our humanness, where we have messed up, made a mistake, let them see our tears at appropriate times, allow them to see that we, too, are human, and doing our best to live as Jesus would expect, but that we are not perfect. Reflect on how often in our programmes we 'teach' the Bible passage instead of allowing the children to explore and figure out meaning for themselves. In our teachings, are we sure we are not taking anything out of context?

Conclusion

Child rights are something which, used with biblical basis and a good emphasis on responsibilities to others in families and community, can be used as a tool to ensure that our children survive, develop and reach their full potential. We have noted that they may be interpreted differently in different cultures, and how, in our increasingly multicultural country, awareness and understanding need to be used.

In addition, a wider understanding of global issues is needed to ensure that as we advocate for children here in the UK, we are also aware of our lifestyle choices and how they impact the life of children we may never meet yet have the ability to affect their lives for good or bad. The Church is in a perfect position to be able to speak out about such things, but this needs to come with a commitment to try to live as much as possible in this mind set, to allow it to change our decisions.

The child's right to participation at the fullest level is also something that churches may need to engage more with, ensuring that their voices are heard in decisions that affect them and in the life of the church in general. They need to be seen as equal members of the Kingdom, with roles to fulfil, to lead others as well as at times being led, to be allowed to use their God-given gifts to edify the congregation, fulfilling their essential role as part of the body of Christ.

However, dangers may abound when the emphasis is placed on ministry to children alone. Much may be lost of intergenerational worth as segregation happens, with different age groups meeting separately. It is my firm belief that if children were fully released in the Kingdom to fulfil their God-given roles, we would see a very different Church today, and even a very different world.

QUESTIONS FOR REFLECTION AND DISCUSSION

- How many child rights do you know? You may be surprised at what is included. Try listing as many as you can, before Googling 'UNCRC' to see what is included. What are the ways that these may be abused or denied in your local setting, as well as nationally and internationally? What responsibilities go with them?

- In your local congregation, how are children able to minister? How many meetings that discuss church life, of which children are a part, are designed to be able to also hear children's voices? Where are the children allowed to minister? To whom are they allowed to minister?

- What are your passions – Clothes? Phones? Chocolate? There are many things that we do not think about when enjoying, yet frequently someone (often a child in foreign lands) may be suffering to provide what we want. In which areas do we need to make changes? What will happen to our lifestyles if we do? Are we willing to sacrifice that?

- Think of your local congregation. How often are the generations able to mix to learn and share with each other? What are the situations in which this happens? If this is not often, what can you do to increase this?

References and further reading

Church of England (2016) *Rooted in the Church.* London: Church of England Education Office.

Collier, J. (2009) 'The United Convention on the Rights of the Child (CRC).' In *Toddling to the Kingdom.* London: The Child Theology Movement.

Griffiths, M. (2009) *One Generation from Extinction.* London: Monarch Books.

Griffiths, M. (2017) *Changing Lives.* London: Monarch Books.

Hart, R. (1992) *Children's Participation: From Tokenism to Citizenship.* Florence: UNICEF. Available at www.unicef-irc.org/publications/pdf/childrens_participation.pdf

Jersak, B. (2003) *Children, Can You Hear Me?* Abbotsford: Fresh Wind Press.

Marshall, K. and Parvis, P. (2004) *Honouring Children.* Edinburgh: St Andrews Press.

Mayor, S. (2017) 'UK children have alarming gap in health between rich and poor, report finds.' *British Medical Journal 356,* j377

Mbiti, J.S. (1969) *African Religions and Philosophy.* Nairobi: Heinemann.

McConnell, D. (2007) 'Being the Family of Faith.' In D. McConnell, J. Orona and P. Stockley (eds) *Understanding God's Heart for Children* (pp.246–251). London: Authentic.

Miles, G. (2003) 'The Purpose of Advocacy for and with Children.' In G. Miles and J.J. Wright (eds) *Celebrating Children* (p.95). Carlisle: Paternoster.

Myers. B. (1999) *Walking with the Poor.* New York: Orbis.

Powell, K. (2007) 'God Welcomes Children Fully into the Family of Faith.' In D. McConnell, J. Orona and P. Stockley (eds) *Understanding God's Heart for Children* (pp.227–237). London: Authentic.

Scott, D. (2007) 'Theological Dignity and Human Rights for Children.' In D. McConnell, J. Orona and P. Stockley (eds) *Understanding God's Heart for Children* (pp.23–31). London: Authentic.

Stephenson, P. (2003) 'The "Rights" of the Child and the Christian Response.' In G. Miles and J.J. Wright (eds) *Celebrating Children* (pp.52–61). Carlisle: Paternoster.

Taber, C. (2002) 'In the Image of God: The Gospel and human rights.' *International Bulletin 26*(3), 98–102.

UN (United Nations) (1989) *Convention on the Rights of the Child.* Available at https://downloads.unicef. org.uk/wp-content/uploads/2010/05/UNCRC_united_nations_convention_on_the_rights_ of_the_child.pdf?_ga=2.216358549.247692187.1537455708-670060270.1537455708

Wall, J. (2017) *Children's Rights: Today's Global Challenge.* London: Rowman & Littlefield.

Wells, K. (2009) *Childhood in a Global Perspective.* Cambridge: Polity Press.

Chapter 12

HARD-NOSED HEAD TEACHER

Michael Wells

Introduction

The training team had carefully set up the room and briefed the participants, then watched in disbelief as chaos broke out: petty squabbles morphed into fights, toys were thrown about, reams of paper scribbled on before being torn into confetti and even pencils snapped in pieces. Appalled, they called a halt, and slowly the room returned to some sort of normality. A comfort break was suggested and as the course participants left, the team began to tidy up and assess how they might recover the situation. It appeared that every single course member was convinced that a six-year-old would behave in this destructive and disruptive manner.

The long-established primary school teacher was given the role by colleagues of being the 'enforcer'. Children who misbehaved as they awaited the head teacher's arrival for assembly each day had to report to the enforcer before returning to their own classroom. Solemnly each name was written in the book, while the ten-year-old class members looked on, exchanging knowing looks. No record was made of the crimes committed: enjoying the ripping sound of Velcro shoe fastenings, talking briefly with a friend or not sitting properly, cross-legged and in a straight line.

A group of lads, self-labelled the 'Custard Creams', after their favourite snack, found it hard to stay on task for any length of time. Their one ambition was to play their favourite game, but even that often degenerated into rancour and argument. Creative tasks were quickly abandoned; their attention during brief five-minute talks quickly wandered. Yet each week they were there for club night, the one space where they felt truly at home.

These three anecdotes introduce this hard-nosed head teacher, and illustrate the scope of this chapter. Despite the caricatures of the six-year-olds portrayed by adults on the training weekend, experience suggests that the majority of children want to be good. Yes, they break the rules, they transgress, but like most adults, they want to conform, to be liked and to work harmoniously with others. Sometimes the problem is not so much the child as the adult who sets the rules, expecting mature behaviour from the immature. My class of ten-year-olds knew that the names written in the book were there merely for form's sake; it was my way of supporting my fellow teachers while ensuring that the miscreants were not treated too harshly. So far as the Custard Creams were concerned, each of them had some sort of diagnosis for behavioural problems.

As a teacher I indeed had my own set of rules, a code of behaviour that I expected to be followed most of the time. I viewed them as pretty basic – one person talking at a time, either me or a pupil, and a proper consideration of the needs of others, including adults. That said, each new group that arrived in my classroom needed to have these rules spelled out for them, usually in the context of a discussion about why they were necessary and what it meant in real terms. Within the state education system it was not appropriate to link them directly to the Ten Commandments, but that was the underpinning structure. This code of conduct ensured that the children I taught were secure in the knowledge that they would not inadvertently fall foul of some unknown regulation, though they knew that some days I might appear more irritable than others. They were also aware that our classroom rules were consistently and appropriately applied. Actually, establishing these limits on acceptable behaviour did take time, but it was not long before a look or even a slight pause helped the children to observe our code.

Good fences make good neighbours

Robert Frost, in his poem 'Mending Wall' (1914), talked about good fences making good neighbours. For many of us, our greatest fear is that of offending people unintentionally, and so sometimes we don't make the most of situations and opportunities for fear of getting it wrong. In the same way, unwritten rules and conventions are a hazard and often a barrier to progress; for example, some Christian communities have no clear rules about the gender of their leadership, but would never consider anyone with two X chromosomes for a leadership role – as there is no rule, there is no possibility of debating it. There is perhaps no need to produce a detailed code. That was something that the Pharisees of Jesus' time chose to do, burdening people unnecessarily with a sense of obligation and guilt, and as Jesus reminds us in Matthew 23.23–27, forgetting the important elements of justice and mercy and faithfulness. In our work with children we do, however, need to be clear just where the boundaries lie.

In his book *The Growth of Love*, Keith White (2008) devotes a whole chapter to boundaries, making the point that children actually need to know what acceptable behaviour is and what it is not. Without boundaries the child's world becomes unpredictable and random, with no understanding of cause and effect. This could well lead to the child feeling out of control, with the risk that this behaviour will be projected on to others. One of the misapprehensions of that training group in the anecdote above was that children automatically misbehave, or perhaps the error was with the trainers who did not explain the ground rules adequately, leaving the course members with no criteria against which to judge their behaviour. It is, therefore, worth spending some time trying to define the boundaries that you consider to be important, and perhaps giving them some sort of priority.

As a teacher I did find the preoccupation of some of my colleagues with children lining up in single file and sitting in straight lines slightly baffling; for me it provided just another rule to be disobeyed. But then, many of them endorsed Christianity as a means of disciplining the children's behaviour, using the fear of God's displeasure to discourage what they perceived as 'bad' behaviour. I tend to fall back on the *treat others as you want to be treated yourself* approach, but even that requires further refining as you consider the age of the children you work with, the setting and how your particular Christian community operates. If you are meeting in a side room during a church service, you may need different standards to a mid-week club in a large hall. But children do need to know what is acceptable and what is not. Establishing boundaries should not be about draconian limits on personal freedom, but about providing a safe framework where children and adults alike are able to share something of their experience of God.

I happily supported my teaching colleagues as they trained younger pupils into acceptable behaviour – until you have actually learned to sit still and listen it is difficult to follow instructions and get the most out of being with other people. My own apparently casual attitude to lining up and walking into assembly in single file was based on the children's previously learned behaviour. As ten- and eleven-year-olds they knew what was expected of them and did not need to be dragooned into single file or exhorted to silence. They were more than ready to exercise self-control and did not require my intervention. The Custard Creams, though significantly older, were not at that stage, and required constant reminders of how to behave towards others. Also, because of their specific needs, some rules were given less significance than others.

As a classroom teacher I was very aware of the fact that I had the advantage of a built-in authority; however, in the voluntary sector this is not necessarily true. For a start the children are there by choice, or parental command. Often the contact is at best once a week for no more than 60 minutes, or possibly once a month for the length of a sermon. Often the pressure is to maintain some kind of order, if not quiet, lest the adults are disturbed, and to teach a very specific scriptural lesson. There is little time to establish a relationship, let alone develop a suitable code of behaviour for an informal group. It is, however, still worth spending some time thinking about how you communicate respect for everyone, children and adults, in the group.

I was much taken by White's suggestion that the entire Church should visit the Ten Commandments at least once a year, reminding everyone of God's instructions for living harmoniously (2008, p.94), rules that apply to adult and child alike. Sometimes it seems that the Church has not yet grasped Jesus' injunction to be childlike, and retains a hierarchical perspective that sees children at the bottom of the pecking order and not an integral part of today's Christian community. Language like 'Sunday School teachers and leaders' can disavow that we are called to work *with* or perhaps *among* children, and often little allowance is given for children to have spiritual insights. Writers like Csinos and Beckwith (2013) help us to explore how we are wrong in perceiving children as empty vessels destined to be filled with doctrinal truths, but this perception often conditions the way that they are treated. Jesus respected children as children – they were not unformed adults, they were individuals. The challenge for those of us who work with children is to see them as individuals and to seek to understand something of their background and experience. Many years ago, a young teenager from a very troubled background, whose behaviour around the church building could be quite disruptive, was a constant visitor in the family home of their Bible class leader. There they were treated with respect and listened to, their opinions valued and discussed. This family setting was key in establishing them as the person God wanted them to be. Here they experienced unconditional love, but were expected to observe the same rules as the rest of the family. Interesting anecdotes and personal insights may be of value, but one of the weaknesses of that approach is that it offers little of immediate and practical value to the harassed volunteer. We all look for answers, so let me suggest some for your consideration.

Setting boundaries

So how might we define the working boundaries that are appropriate for our group? A good starting point is to think of your own life experiences and prejudices. These will inevitably colour the way that you see things, and being aware of petty prejudices guards against them becoming significant issues as we get acquainted with the group. Hopefully you will already have your own code of expected behaviour and know what sort of things irritate you. This is where your judgement comes in and you have to decide what is significant and what is no more than your personal preference. Much depends on your own attitude to the group – your understanding of what your role is, and your sense of play and its role in spiritual development (Edwards 2011). At one end of the scale you may see yourself as an imparter of wisdom, a source of knowledge and adult authority, while at the other extreme you might feel it right to be just 'one of the gang'. As with most things it is a question of balance – as an adult you have been given responsibility and there are certain expectations that come with that role. Yet in God's upside-down Kingdom children are our model. It may help to think of your group as pilgrims travelling together – you have been on the road before so have experience, but equally the child may have fresh insights and understanding.

From the outset it is worth establishing simple ground rules, perhaps nothing more basic than one voice at a time. With younger children you might use a cuddly toy that is passed about, giving an individual permission to speak, including yourself. It's a new group, and once you have introduced yourself, introduce Ethel, your camel, for example. She will be passed from one child to another and when she is in their hands, they give their name and one simple fact about themselves: 'My name's Suzie, and I've got a pet hamster.' Nine- and ten-year-olds may find the camel a bit of a problem, but early teens may well respond positively. You may have to prompt and encourage some and gently stop others from giving a full life history. A process like this establishes several important principles: you are interested in each individual, everyone has a right to be listened to and no one person is more significant than another.

In many school classrooms there is a list of rules of behaviour that the children have agreed; this may not be appropriate in your setting, but as each situation emerges, it is right to deal with it there and then. When children find it difficult to share resources without petty squabbles, you may want to talk about taking turns and helping each other. Over recent years the fashion of awarding certificates and stickers for positive achievements has gained prominence. This frequently results in the more able child being discriminated against while those who struggle are seen to be rewarded for simply making the effort. While there is no harm in rewarding positive attitudes, it can foster a false motivation where receiving the reward is all that counts, and not how you achieved it. And there are those who delight in failure; after all, if you are unlikely to win the best-behaved award, why not go for the very worst? Scottie May has written an interesting theological reflection on this in Michael Anthony's book. If you do choose to use some sort of positive reward scheme, think carefully about motivating the whole group, and perhaps just run it for a short period, so that it doesn't simply become a stale and therefore useless convention.

The suggestion that the whole Church should revisit the Ten Commandments is perhaps a good starting point. But as I hinted earlier, there is a danger of using this as a blunt weapon – simply presenting God's wrath as the ultimate deterrent, though they rarely applied it to their own lives. We need to model the message, showing, by our care and concern for others, how God's rules for living in community work out in daily life. There is a narrative that I find very disturbing in the second book of Kings (2.23–24). Here a group of boys tormented God's messenger Elisha and were punished by being mauled by bears. If we chose, we could use this to exhort our children to good behaviour, but I am not convinced it would be that effective. First, because of the lack of bears, but also because it presents a one-dimensional view of a God of wrath. Our God is a God of loving discipline – why else would David say, 'Even when I walk through the darkest valley, I will not be afraid, for you are close beside me. Your rod and your staff protect and comfort me' (Psalm 23.4)? He provides us with a stout staff to offer protection from wild beasts that threaten as well as comfort from the shepherd's rod – a device to set boundaries, keep the sheep safe and maintain proper discipline.

As a classroom teacher I was frequently called out of the room to deal with some external matter, often nothing more than a computer failing to boot up correctly. This left my lively class unsupervised, but I never really had any qualms about turning my back on them, as my aim was to help them learn self-discipline, not just an adult-inspired code of behaviour. I would make time to talk about what boundaries were appropriate, and I might point out that there was very little challenge in being silly if I was not there – much better they waited until I returned. Most of the time my faith in their common sense was justified and they happily remained on task. With our own children, my wife and I operated a similar system – when the children were young we used walking reins, not to limit their freedom, but to keep them safe. As they grew older and it was appropriate for the family to join me on an away preaching engagement, we would talk through what we expected of them, especially if we were invited to lunch with folk we did not know, and provide them with a set of behavioural cues. A certain look meant 'think about what you are doing', as it may not be the most sensible action, while a slight shake of the head meant an absolute 'no'. We had no intention of embarrassing them in public, and they never let themselves down. We were in the process of training our children to be self-controlled. So long as boundaries are only enforced by an external power, the child is not really free to express themselves; once they are part of their own life values, then they can experience real freedom.

We, as adults, do have a responsibility to consider why a group or individuals react as they do. Is it possible that we are being boring? That they are so familiar with the biblical narrative that it has little meaning? Or are they being rebellious about simply being there when all of their friends are having fun? As individuals we all have different boredom thresholds, and mine is particularly low. Nigel Forde, in his poem in the video that accompanied the Church of England report *Children in the Way*, describes a child banished to the church annexe to cut up bits of paper and map the Holy Land in the time of Jesus who, then 'draws another leper, feels; like him rejected'. While change just for the sake of change is not necessarily a good thing, we do need to be wary of slipping into routines that of themselves are tedious and unproductive. Children undoubtedly benefit from a consistency of approach and treatment, but do not require the same pattern repeated indefinitely. Like adults, they have different learning preferences: some are active, learning through doing; others prefer being told stories or to investigate things for themselves. If our programme contains different elements, we should be able to keep a divergent group engaged.

Very few churches are likely to have a fire-raiser among their children, but I do know of someone who would lock themselves in an upstairs toilet, set light to pieces of toilet paper and then float them out of the window. This usually went unnoticed, so as a final coda they would climb out of the window and lower themselves to the ground, leaving behind a locked toilet to baffle the caretaker. It was not just a sense of adventure that fuelled this particular arsonist; they had been abandoned to the care of Barnardo's aged two, then later placed with a totally unsuitable family, where they suffered even more emotional and physical abuse. This was a very needy child, starved of genuine affection and expected to repay the generosity of their adopted parents by caring for them as they grew older. Fortunately, the church family provided stability and understanding and a safe environment, where the child was able to flourish and take on responsibility. Here was a child who always wanted to be good, but, endued with a lively sense of the ridiculous, just got into mischief and would often take foolish risks. It was the combination of known boundaries and selfless love that helped heal this damaged child, but it was not an easy or straightforward task.

In one church I was working with a group of sub-teens, and despite my very best endeavours, our weekly sessions did not always go to plan. There were all sorts of different factors at work, and one of them was what I label *minister's child syndrome*. Somehow this individual felt that none of the rules applied to them and they had the right to torment and tease anyone they chose. It was little more than a blatant demand for attention and an attempt to dominate all of our activities. As a group we tried every strategy we could think of, but in the end we tacitly agreed to ignore all but the very worst outbursts. For obvious reasons the ultimate sanction of suspension from the group was never an option. I learned a lot about patience and self-control, but still breathed a sigh of relief when this individual finally moved out of the group.

The Custard Creams, though similar in some ways, are quite different; they all have a formal diagnosis of some sort of behavioural problem, but this does not absolve them of any responsibility. I once worked with somebody who would constantly excuse their behaviour with the phrase, 'I've got brain damage', a statement that was genuinely true, but often used in place of an apology or an attempt to ameliorate their behaviour. While it was right to take into account the problems that the lads had, this was not allowed to take precedence over the establishment of appropriate boundaries. They had to learn to curb their exuberance, begin to treat each other more generously, and learn to listen. Working with them is exhausting; it demands huge amounts of patience, the ability to adapt the programme to fit their immediate needs, and a resilient sense of humour, not to mention a good supply of biscuits.

Many years ago an experienced colleague told the story of a mission meeting that was plagued by a very disruptive group of youngsters. He was fast running out of ideas of how he might engage their interest, and then came a light bulb moment. He prayed, but what he went on to say was very different from what I expected. His prayer was very simply, 'Lord help me not to notice', and perhaps that was where we ought to have started this discussion. If we are indeed engaged in work for God, then it is only right to ask him for the help and support that we need: wisdom in framing appropriate and age-relevant boundaries; patience in managing the needs of different individuals; gentleness in coping with those who try our patience; confidence in God's love for each member of our group, including ourselves; God's grace to truly love each person for who they are today; and perhaps the greatest gift required for anyone who seeks to share God's Kingdom – a sense of humour.

Some of us who work with children relish a lively group that will challenge and question, that will debate and discuss, while some of us find this more demanding. Whatever our own preference, we can all choose to allow the children to cause us to reflect on our own beliefs and practices, as they often have a way of looking at things that is quite novel. We need to remind ourselves that Jesus commended children as our model. His words to Nicodemus were, 'you must be born again' (John 3.3), but to his disciples he said, 'Let the little children come to me, and do not hinder them, for the kingdom of God belongs to such as these. Truly I tell you, anyone who will not receive the kingdom of God like a little child will never enter it' (Mark 10.14–15). Perhaps the greatest challenge of working with children is in shedding the prejudices of the adult world, and adopting the curiosity and exploration of childhood.

QUESTIONS FOR REFLECTION AND DISCUSSION

- What is it that you as an individual are trying to achieve with the children you are working with?

- How well do you know your group? Are there any in the group who are showing signs of being especially needy? To what extent are you aware of each individual's own story?

- Read John 4.1–20. How might you have born witness to God's love in that situation? Reflect on what it might have to say about rules, boundaries and priorities.

References and further reading

Anthony, M. (2006) *Perspectives on Children's Spiritual Formation*. Nashville, TN: Broadman and Holman.

Brown, S. and Langtree, A. (2011) *Top Tips on Dealing with Challenging Behaviour*. Bletchley: Scripture Union.

Csinos, D. and Beckwith, I. (2013) *Children's Ministry in the Way of Jesus*. Downers Grove, IL: IVP (Inter-Varsity Press).

Edwards, C. (2011) *Slugs and Snails and Puppy Dogs' Tails: Helping Boys Connect with God*. Leicester: IVP (Inter-Varsity Press).

Frost, R. (1914) 'Mending Wall.' In *North of Boston*. London: David Nutt. Available at www.poetryfoundation.org/poems/44266/mending-wall

Pimlott, J. and Pimlott, N. (2005) *Responding to Challenging Behaviour*. Cambridge: Grove Books.

White, K.J. (2008) *The Growth of Love*. Abingdon: Bible Reading Fellowship.

Chapter 13

FALLING LEAF CATCHER

Experiencing Awe and Wonder with Children

David M. Csinos

Introduction

For the better part of the last decade, I've been instigating a movement in ministry with children and youth through an organisation called Faith Forward.[1] Conceived through a conversation over lunch and birthed through the 'Children, Youth, and a New Kind of Christianity' Conference in 2012, Faith Forward has become a leading network of progressive, innovative and thoughtful practitioners in ministry with children and youth. Our gatherings have welcomed delegates from over three-dozen denominational traditions and from across the US and Canada, as well as Britain, Australia, New Zealand and continental Europe. By joining together across geographic, socio-economic and denominational lines, we have forged creative and courageous ideas for engaging in faith formation with young people.

One thing I've learned from my work with Faith Forward is that leaders in ministry with children and youth too often exert so much time and energy in organising formational experiences for the young people in their congregations and communities that they end up neglecting their own faith in the process. So, in response to this reality, at our 2014 gathering in Nashville, Tennessee we asked Mark Yaconelli to lead an exercise intended to help us reconnect to the God that we have all encountered at different moments in our lives. After guiding us through a process of recollecting a moment when we encountered a sacred presence – a remembering of this moment – Yaconelli (2014) called us to see these moments as wells in the landscape of our lives:

---

1 www.faith-forward.net

They're wellsprings. And you can go back to them and still draw water. There is still more to be given in those places… We have these moments of an in-breaking, where the kingdom of God is suddenly here, right now. And all the brokenness dissipates, just for an instant. And the invisible world becomes visible. It shows up and we know it.

About ten years before hearing Yaconelli say this at Faith Forward 2014, I found myself sitting in on a class about missions and evangelism at a small Christian college in Canada. At one point in the session, the professor called students to become missionaries in their community, people who help their friends and neighbours understand a particular theological interpretation of Jesus' death that was deemed to be necessary for receiving God's gift of salvation. To this end, one student made a presentation about the 'bridge approach' to evangelism, which essentially states that we human beings are on one side of a chasm, separated from God, who rests on the other side. The infinitely deep chasm that keeps us disconnected from God, the student said, is sin. But, he went on, Jesus' death on the cross created a bridge that we can choose to cross and be with God. Conveniently, the cross fitted perfectly in the chasm on the diagram that the student drew on the chalkboard.

I have never understood why this understanding of sin and redemption appeared to portray God as some sort of immobile object that never crossed the bridge to be with us. While the Psalmist metaphorically proclaims that 'The Lord is my rock' (Psalm 18.2), this explanation of the cross seemed to make God into literal rock, a mighty boulder that could not be moved. This God didn't even make the effort to meet us halfway across the bridge!

If I have to be honest, I think these sorts of evangelistic tactics are embarrassing. In fact, I was writing about this experience as I sat on a crowded commuter train leaving London at the end of a busy workday. As the man sitting next to me glanced over at my screen, he discreetly put in his earbuds and played some music that was loud enough to say to me, 'Please don't tell me about how my sins are a chasm between me and God.' These sorts of strategies have never seemed to me to be effective ways to bring people to faith. It's odd to expect that we can convince people of God's love through rational argument. But isn't this what we do with children so often? Through curriculum, object lessons, crafts, skits and games, children's ministry has pointed faith formation toward teaching children *about* the Bible and *about* God. Even leaders who might disagree with this cognitive-based, rational approach to formation sometimes rely on these approaches simply because they don't know what else to do with young people. So they tend to keep relying on approaches like this and others that they don't actually believe in. Many of us suspect – and are even convinced – that faith is so much more than theological propositions like that taught through the chasm metaphor. But we don't know what else to do.

I must admit that I have a love–hate relationship to the Church. I love God, even in my moments of doubt and those dark nights of the soul. But I don't always love God's Church. We can be an arrogant, stubborn and ornery bunch. And no rational argument for God's love would have ever kept me in the Church, that broad family of God, all this time. I've remained part of this worldwide communion of sinners and saint and I've continued to try to follow Jesus because I've had first-hand experiences of God. Those moments of sacred presence that Yaconelli called into my memory in Nashville remind me that I know of God's love, not because someone explained it to me through a convincing argument, but because I have encountered God at different times in my life. God's Spirit has touched my spirit. These wellsprings and these wellsprings alone have convinced me to continue the journey of discipleship.

What would happen if we allowed these wellsprings to become the centrepieces of ministry with children? What power does standing in awe and wonder in the sacred presence of God – however we perceive or understand that presence – hold for the journey of faith? What would happen if we who are leaders went back to these wellsprings ourselves? This chapter is a sojourn through these sorts of questions.

Born this way

In the field of children's spirituality, few works rival Hay and Nye's *The Spirit of the Child* (2006) as central for understanding the spiritual lives of young people. Although more than 20 years old, this text continues to remain paramount for its assertion that spirituality is an inherent, biological aspect of the human condition and best understood in children as what Nye calls 'relational consciousness', an innate awareness of their connections to themselves, others, the world around them, and ultimately, to God. Through her research among children in British primary schools, Nye found that spirituality in children 'was recognized by a distinctive property of mental activity, profound and intricate enough to be termed "consciousness", and remarkable for its confinement to a broadly relational, inter- and intra-personal domain' (Hay with Nye 2006, p.109).

Many scholars and practitioners of ministry with children may be quite familiar with the idea that spirituality is inherent to human life, and human childhood in particular. It has been a pivotal assumption in my own research into spiritual styles, children's ministry and children's theological meaning-making (Csinos 2011, 2007; Csinos and Beckwith 2013). But when it comes to the ways in which we engage in faith formation with children, I wonder how seriously we actually take this assertion. Do we act like we really believe that children have spiritual capacities simply because they are human beings?

If we do, then we need to admit that maybe we've been going about ministry with children in the wrong way. For too long, ministry with children has focused on teaching children particular theological facts or interpretations of biblical stories. I recently asked my students in a graduate-level course to critically analyse children's ministry curricula. While evaluating this assignment, I noticed a particular trend: regardless of the theological, pedagogical or contextual dynamics at play within the resource, each curriculum had as a key goal the imparting of particular 'points' or 'truths' to children. Not one of them focused on helping children to have encounters with God and making meaning of these experiences. This is not to say, of course, that there aren't any resources out there that nurture the spiritual experiences of children. But the great majority of curricula tend to assume that what matters most for faith formation in young disciples is the acquisition of particular cognitive-based assertions.

What would it mean, however, if we took seriously Hay and Nye's position that children are inherently spiritual beings? It would mean that we'd need to re-think the common practice of focusing on filling children with head-knowledge and assuming this will lead them to love God, both now and throughout their lives. Maybe we don't need to teach children about God or convince them of God's love for them because they already experience it. Maybe they already know about God's love because they sense a connection to some sort of sacred presence, even if they don't articulate it or name it as a God-moment.

Childhood openness

Hay and Nye certainly aren't the first to promote the idea the young people are somehow inherently connected with God. As he was walking throughout Judea and the surrounding area, Jesus met some people who were bringing children to him so that he could bless them. I'm sure if you're reading this book that you know this story, which is told in all three synoptic Gospels (Matthew 19.13–15; Mark 10.13–16; Luke 18.15–17). Jesus' disciples attempted to have the children taken away from Jesus, but Jesus said, 'Let the little children come to me, and do not hinder them, for the kingdom of God belongs to such as these. Truly I tell you, anyone who will not receive the kingdom of God like a little child will never enter it' (Mark 10.14–15). And then the writer of Mark's Gospel goes so far as to tell us that Jesus actually lifts the children into his arms and blesses them.

Jesus held up children not only as members of the Kingdom, but also as exemplars of what it means to be a member of God's reign. Young people, Jesus says, are our models of faith, the ones who seem to instinctively know who he is, simply by virtue of the fact that they are children. New Testament Scholar Judith Gundry argues that it is children's dependence on God – their inability to live under the law, as 'non-doers of the law' (2008, p.169) to use her words – that makes them prime examples of Kingdom heirs: '*only* those who stand in the least palatable, most shameful and unenviable position of dependence on God, namely, that of a little child, will enter the kingdom of God – and therefore *anyone* can enter it' (2008, p.172; original emphasis). Gundry goes on to posit that while some first-century-hearers would have seen this requirement as unappealing, it is, in fact, truly liberation, for it flings wide the doors of the Kingdom to all people, regardless of their status under the law (2008, p.172). This dependency on God is tied up with relationship; by being in relationship with God, by encountering sacred presence in all their vulnerability, are children – and all of us – dependent on God.

Two millennia after Jesus' bold claim that children are exemplars of those who can enter God's Kingdom, twentieth-century-Catholic theologian Karl Rahner wrote about aspects of childhood that make them inherently connected with God. Rahner paints an image of childhood as intrinsically valuable in itself and not simply as a necessary stage to pass through on the way to adolescence and adulthood. Childhood, he writes, 'has a direct relationship with God. It touches upon the absolute divinity of God not only as maturity, adulthood and the later phases of life touch upon this, but rather in a special way of its own' (Rahner 1971, p.36).

For Rahner, human childhood is characterised theologically as 'infinite openness' (1971, p.48). We are all born with a fundamental transcendence, a going-beyond the horizons of the here-and-now. In fact, our adult lives are a quest to once again find that infinite openness that eventually becomes more finite and less open as we make our way through life. According to Rahner, childhood:

> …must take the form of trust, of openness, of expectation, of readiness to be controlled by another, of interior harmony with the unpredictable forces with which the individual finds himself confronted. It must manifest

itself as freedom…as receptivity, as hope which is still not disillusioned. This is the childhood that must be present and active as an effective force at the very roots of our being… [T]he childhood which belongs to the child in the biological sense is only the beginning, the prelude, the foretaste and the promise of this other childhood, which is the childhood proved and tested and at the same time assailed, which is present in the mature man. In other words, we must take childhood in this *latter* sense as the true and proper childhood, the fullness of that *former* childhood, the childhood of immaturity. (1971, p.47; emphasis added)

Rahner holds that childhood contains within itself characteristics that place human beings in a direct relationship with God. Openness, dependence, trust – these are all dependent on whether we encounter that to which we are open, on which we depend, and in whom we trust. All work together to give children an inherent '*orientation to God*' (Rahner 1971, p.48; emphasis added).

There's a story that's been attributed to a number of different people over the past few years. I'm not sure who told it first. It's tells about a little girl who had recently become a big sister. At one point, shortly after the birth of her new brother, she asked her parents for some time alone with the infant. Not sure what to do, they left the room but listened in from just outside the closed door. They heard their daughter walk over to the newborn child and whisper, 'Baby, tell me what God is like. I'm starting to forget.'

If we truly believe that Jesus, Rahner and this little girl are right, if we believe that children possess an innate connection with God, then they don't need to learn about God so much as they need to encounter God. Of course, we all experience God differently, and some people might know God when they *know about* God, and this is something that I expand on in my description of word-centred spirituality in *Children's Ministry that Fits: Beyond One-Size-Fits.* For far too long, however, common approaches to children's formation have assumed that if we only teach young people the right things, they'll come to know God. What would happen if instead of teaching children about God, we created contexts in which they could have encounters with God? Of course, we cannot control where and when God shows up in young people's lives, but as my friend Alan Charter, who heads up the charity Home for Good, said to me in a recent conversation, the main question for children's spiritual formation is, 'What can I do to facilitate as many God-encounters as possible?' The rest is up to the God we trust to show up.

Falling leaves

So what does all this mean? If, as I have argued, children are hard-wired with an innate spirituality, if they have a natural tendency to connect with God, if the societies in which we live tend to stifle these aspect of our lives as we grow older, and if the theological journey is one of becoming a child again – if we assume all of these things, we need to admit that perhaps we've got things backwards. Maybe instead of adults teaching children how to be Christian, they're the ones who should be teaching us.

As beings made to be open to connections with God, we could argue that children are, in fact, more attuned to finding wellsprings, those encounters with sacred presence, than we adults are. Not only do Hay and Nye call attention to the inherency of spirituality among younger people, but they also argue that our 'adults worlds' actually stifle our natural relational consciousness (Hay with Nye 2006, p.33). The world around us – and we could claim that the Church is also indicted in this argument – is often structured in ways that make that inherent divine spark within each of us grow increasingly dim. That consciousness of our relationships, which is central to Hay and Nye's concept of spirituality, increasingly becomes a collection of memories to those things that we were once connected with in far greater and less adulterated manners.

We are all creatures made to catch God's Spirit as it falls on us like autumn leaves. While we're children, we might see these leaves cascading to the ground, grab our nets, and run outside, trying to catch as many of them as we can. But as life goes on, our orientation to the world changes. We become less likely to play outside where the leaves fall, and we might not stop as we pass by windows to see the wind blowing the leaves where she wills. But this does not mean the leaves stop falling; it simply means that we neglect to notice them or stand in awe as they dance about in the air around us. God's Spirit still reaches out to us. Jesus still waits for us at the wellsprings of our lives, saying, 'I am he, the one who is speaking to you' (John 4.26). Will we stop to notice?

When we do pause to catch a few of these leaves, we might find that they are the real stuff of faith, the reason that any of us continue to try living as disciples of Jesus. And we might realise that the journey of faith among children and adults is not as different as we are often led to believe. If we shift our focus from teaching children about God to helping them experience God and name those moments when they catch God's Spirit, we realise that we all walk a common pilgrimage. If, as my friend has said, our role is to facilitate as many God-encounters as possible, then we can widen the path for the journey, for there are no age restrictions, no prerequisite knowledge, ability or personality required to experiencing God.

So as you continue to nurture faith in children, think back to those moments when you have encountered sacred presence. Recall the wellsprings of your life where God has shown up. And remember the wisdom of Mark Yaconelli (2014), who reminds us that:

> ...this is the very same God that Jesus knew. And you know this God. Not believe in. You *know* this God. You have encountered this God. Who would you be if every day you allowed this presence to come and be with you? Who would you be if you remembered these moments before you went out to be with your family, your friends, your community, your co-workers. What kind of courage would you carry?

Being a disciple of Jesus is difficult work. And being part of the body of Christ isn't always as easy a journey. Are you where you are today, in your current vocation and mission, as a member of God's Church, because somebody convinced you about God? Or are you a committed follower because you encountered God? If my hunch is correct, then let's use this as a reason to go out into our ministries with children and facilitate as many God-encounters as possible. Yes, the young people in our faith communities do well to learn about Scripture and theology and tradition, but that will come over time. What would it mean to take Jesus' words seriously? What would it look like if we actually believed that children are capable of having deep Spirit-to-spirit encounters with God? Despite everything we do to nurture faith in children, do we really trust that God will show up?

QUESTIONS FOR REFLECTION AND DISCUSSION

- When has God shown up in your life? Take a moment to silently recall when you sensed a sacred presence, and reflect on how this moment shaped your view of and relationship with God.

- If children are more inclined to be open to God-encounters, how can they remind us to slow down and pay attention to experiences of God in our own lives?

- How can you help children to name their encounters with God and share them with others?

- How can children's work be re-envisioned to better facilitate and reflect on God-encounters?

References and further reading

Berryman, J.W. (2017) *Becoming Like a Child: The Curiosity and Maturity Beyond the Norm*. New York: Church Publishing.

Csinos, D.M. (2007) 'The Biblical theme of welcoming children.' *McMaster Journal of Theology and Ministry 8*, 97–117.

Csinos, D.M. (2011) *Children's Ministry that Fits: Beyond One-Size-Fits-All Approaches to Nurturing Children's Spirituality*. Eugene, OR: Wipf & Stock.

Csinos, D.M. and Beckwith, I. (2013) *Children's Ministry in the Way of Jesus*. Downers Grove, IL: IVP (Inter-Varsity Press).

Hay, D. with Nye, R. (2006) *The Spirit of the Child* (rev. edn). London: Jessica Kingsley Publishers.

Gundry, J.M. (2008) 'Children in the Gospel of Mark, with Special Attention to Jesus' Blessing of the Children (Mark 10:13–16) and the Purpose of Mark.' In M.J. Bunge, T.E. Fretheim and B.R. Gaventa (eds) *The Child in the Bible* (pp.143–176). Grand Rapids, MI: Eerdmans.

May, S., Posterski, B., Stonehouse, C. and Cannell, L. (2005) *Children Matter: Celebrating Their Place in the Church, Family, and Community*. Grand Rapids, MI: Eerdmans.

Nye, R. (2009) *Children's Spirituality: What It Is and Why It Matters*. London: Church House Publishing.

Rahner, K. (1971) 'Ideas for a Theology of Childhood.' In *Theological Investigations*, Vol. VII. New York: Herder & Herder.

Yaconelli, M. (2003) *Dangerous Wonder: The Adventure of Childlike Faith*. Colorado Springs, CO: NavPress.

Yaconelli, M. (2014) 'Presentation at Faith Forward 2014.' Nashville, TN, 19–22 May.

Chapter 14

PERSPECTIVES ON CHILD THEOLOGY

Keith J. White

Introduction

This chapter is a description of a personal journey of discovery in a field that has become known as Child Theology. On the way there were new insights and new companions drawn from every continent. It seems to me rather like the logbook of a ship or diary of a traveller. My hope is that it will serve to connect with what the other writers in this volume are saying, and with the contexts and issues that readers are encountering in their relationships with children in the name of Jesus.

Just one preliminary word of clarification: this brief log does not purport to be a summary of the story of the Child Theology Movement. Although it interweaves with this wider story and has been greatly blessed and informed by it, the focus for now is on a personal journey. So a few words about my background and what I was doing before the journey began may help to set this brief record in context.

I was born in an unusual household in the East End of London. Because my family, including grandparents and parents, had been caring for children in need since 1899, I grew up with about 40 sisters and brothers (not related to me by blood, but sharing an extensive amount of our childhoods). These siblings came from very different backgrounds, and so I was exposed to a wide range of views, assumptions and cultures from an early age. The home is called Mill Grove.

It is a Christian household, where I was taught the Scriptures, Christian songs and choruses and the biographies of Christians around the world. I attended church regularly and took part in church activities, but the inclusive nature of the household, and its many connections with congregations of quite different traditions, meant that I never felt exclusively attached to or part of a particular denomination or Christian group. I now give thanks that I have drunk deeply from the waters of quite different expressions of the Christian faith, as well as from other traditions and faiths.

For most of my life I have continued to live at Mill Grove, and for over 40 years I have been the father of the extended family and leader of the community. Over this time most of what I have studied and written has been motivated by a desire to understand the children I was living with better: their feelings, the effects of separation and loss, their relationships, family patterns, generational characteristics, learning and faith.

Lastly I have been studying and exploring theology for most of my life, not as part of a formal course of study (though I have taught it), but as I was impelled to wrestle with thorny questions, and discovered fellow travellers experiencing similar challenges in real life.

So it is that I have been engaged in 'children's work' for most of my life, and always in the name of Jesus and as part of his body, the Church. For this reason, 'child' and 'theology' have always been interacting with one another consciously or unconsciously in my heart and soul.

The Bible and children

The project known now as Child Theology began in a tangible way for me when I was asked to speak at a conference in De Bron, Holland, in 2001. It was an international gathering of Christians engaged in various forms of activity with, and for, children. The seriousness of their work, and the commitment of the workers and their organisations, was never in doubt. But there was a nagging question about the depth of biblical and theological roots nourishing the activity. It so happened that not long before the conference there was an excellent reader prepared for Tearfund by Paul Stephenson and the late Judith Ennew, two long-standing friends and colleagues of mine (Ennew and Stephenson 2000). It was designed as background reading for a workshop in Cambridge held at the Centre for Family Research on 8 December 2000. An early section of this reader caught my eye: '[The Framework] explores what the Bible has to say about children and God's character. Unlike much Western culture in the twentieth century, the cultural context of the Bible is not child-centred. In fact, the Bible says very little about children' (Ennew and Stephenson 2000, p.3). This provided an underlying challenge for my paper. Without reference works to hand and having re-read as much of the Bible as I could in preparation for the talk, I discovered that there was, in fact, a considerable amount in the Bible about, and sometimes addressed directly to, children and young people. The paper, 'Rediscovering Children at the Heart of Mission', was published and re-published from then until the time of writing in 2017. It was in two parts: a survey of biblical material about children, and a suggested theological framework for exploring how God in Christ relates to children. To this day the first part has received probably overdue attention, while the second has still not been seriously discussed!

The relation between the Bible and children has been a major strand of the journey ever since, up to and including the book *Entry Point*, a study of just one passage of Scripture, Matthew 18 (Willmer and White 2013). Many others have written on the subject, and this is not the place to attempt a bibliography of their views and conclusions. One of those who has done much helpful work in this area is my friend and colleague, Marcia Bunge (2001, 2008). Many of us have found her two edited collections indispensable mines of historical information, and biblical commentary, respectively. It is now accepted that the Bible does have a lot to say about children, and that Christian writers have written extensively about their various understandings of the Bible and children.

As I have studied the works of others, and written regularly myself, however, it has become apparent to me that there is a fundamental issue whenever we approach the Scriptures with a single category or question in mind. Let me hasten to add that coming with pressing, practical, real-life concerns is probably the best way into the heart of God and His Word. But in the process the questions and the assumptions that lay behind them are likely to be challenged, even deconstructed, with new shapes and configurations emerging. What do we mean, for example, by saying that 'humans are made in the image of God'? Is that about each individual human being, young and old? Or is it about human being (that is, every part of the human race)? Do children have a uniquely privileged place, or are they part of humanity as a whole? Is there a risk of being partisan in our advocacy of children at the expense of other aspects of human being? What are the commonalities between those who do theology with a focus on children, and those who do theology with a focus on people with a disability (Young 2014)? When is the Bible referring to actual children (of a certain age), and when are the words 'child' or 'little ones' symbols or signs of other people and other subjects? The phrase 'children of Israel' is one of the most obvious examples.

Since 2001 the overriding lesson I have learned is that I must be willing to let go of my own agenda, work and sense of agency, if I am to be genuinely in a position to hear God speak. This has nothing to do with letting go of the burning questions: very much the reverse, in fact. The journey has been a long and surprising one. I am no less involved with or committed to children, but I try to be more enquiring and receptive as I open the Scriptures, preach and pray. The shift has been from a focus on asking for God's blessing on my/our activities towards an attitude that is seeking to hear the voice of God in Christ, and to pray that His will might be done. Often I am left with little sense of what might be called an 'answer'. It's a surprising, lively, unpredictable experience. Is it perhaps a child's hopefulness and openness to the future that has been one of the keys?

Child development theory

When we speak of 'child' or 'childhood', there is also the question of what we mean by these words. The sociology of childhood is burgeoning and contested. The attempt to connect biblical usages of the terms with contemporary children and childhood reveals substantive hermeneutical challenges. It is pretty much accepted that understandings of children have changed fundamentally over the centuries. An aspect of this general issue is child development theory. One of the many discoveries along the way has been the power that contemporary child development theory has in shaping the ways in which individuals and institutions understand and relate to children right across the board: from parents to teachers, doctors, ministers, psychologists, writers and children's workers. The way local church is conceived and constructed often reflects this prevailing discourse, and the whole area of faith formation seems to be set within this dominant paradigm. Put simply, the current concept of child development conceives of a series of steps of progress from birth to adulthood and maturity: onwards and upwards! Diagrams that portray this are universally popular, as I have learned to my cost when trying to critique them as a teacher!

It takes a good deal of insight and courage to question the whole basis of this model: whether on account of its accuracy when tested by real human experience of life and childhood on the one hand, or biblical wisdom and Christian theology on the other; the more so because it is buttressed by a liberal meta-narrative of human progress, and the powerful influences of marketing. It was only on discovering the pioneering work of James E. Loder (1995) that I began to find a better, and more holistic, way of conceiving of child development deeply rooted in observation of real children, a profound understanding of professional theory and a theologically informed understanding of the human condition as contingent on God in Christ.

Unless and until this powerful paradigm of development is questioned and modified, there is a risk that everything Christians and churches do that relates to children will tend to be moulded by contemporary orthodoxy. A good practical example would be faith formation, made famous in Christian circles by Dr James Fowler's *Stages of Faith* (1981).

Whether one takes the biblical record of how people encounter the living God, or Christian theology of revelation, it is hard to keep intact any idea of a progression of predictable stages! This has profound if not explosive implications for how we understand everything, from secular learning and schooling to 'faith formation', 'church', 'Christian education' and Christian parenting. I am now convinced that Loder offers a compelling starting point for critiquing and re-orientating the existing model. Like him, the journey has taken me way out of my 'comfort zone' and into seemingly strange ways of understanding God's dealings with humankind.

Children's mission and ministry

From the time of 'Rediscovering Children at the Heart of Mission' until 2015, when co-editing *Theology, Mission and Child: Global Perspectives* (Prevette *et al.* 2014), children's mission and ministry were never far from my thoughts. Placing them side-by-side reveals a thread in the journey of discovery and change in which I have been engaged. The second part of the original paper attempted to set mission with children within the life of Jesus Christ from birth to Ascension and the Second Coming. The centre of the latter book is a chapter that I co-authored with Haddon Willmer, which focuses on the death and resurrection of Jesus as the heart of mission. If mission is cruciform, then all Christians and Christian organisations that engage in mission in the name of Jesus must face the possibility of failure and defeat as they hold fast to their calling in Christ Jesus. The death and resurrection of Jesus are inseparable in the process of Christian life and witness.

We cannot guarantee 'success' (a completely non-biblical word in this context) by espousing the best method and securing the necessary human and financial resources. What is more, human agency and effort can never secure 'transformation' in the sense of, say, healing and salvation. These are the preserve or the gift of God in Christ by His Spirit. Far from being a counsel of despair, this is one of the great blessings of Christian theology. Mission is not primarily about what we do as followers, even as apostles of Jesus Christ, but about what God is doing and has been doing since before the foundation of the world.

We are at best servants of this process, sometimes creating the space for the work of God's Spirit, sometimes operating in the (kenotic) space that God has created in Christ, but always as partners called and chosen by God to be part of the body of Christ.

Children's spirituality and children's theology

Much of what has been going on alongside children in the name of Jesus in the past two decades is connected with what is often termed 'children's spirituality'. There have been many books on the subject, notably Hay and Nye's (1998), regular international conferences and many initiatives that draw from and contribute to this thinking (for example, the Spiritual Development Project of Frontier Youth Trust, Godly Play and Messy Church, to name but a few). I have been blessed by my engagement with all of these, yet all the time I have struggled with two elements of what is going on. The first is the very concept of 'spirituality' (that is, in general, and also when applied specifically to children). Whereas when using the term 'spirit' it is possible to find some basis for discussion in both secular thinking and Christian theology, 'spirituality' always tends be amorphous and indescribable. The second element concerns the inner world of a 'child'. Because this is also a mystery (to the child and to an observer, however attuned and skilled), there is a potentially risky and confusing mix of concepts and ideas. It is my interim conclusion (work in progress) that these owe rather more to the Romantic idea of childhood described memorably by, say, Wordsworth, than Christian theology, or studies of actual children and young people.

An aspect of this is the way some of the ideas and practices of children are adumbrated in books, and also on social media. It is assumed by some of those attracted to children's spirituality that children have exceptional contributions to make to Christian thinking and practice. Now, it is axiomatic to a Christian understanding of God's nature and his Kingdom that anything or anyone that He calls and inspires may bring wholly unexpected and unpredicted insights and blessings. Psalm 8.2 is a very relevant case in point. But this is about God being God, not one human category being more important than any other.

As I have already mentioned, I have been blessed by the prayers, the writings, the play and the presence of children (perhaps as much as anyone else I know, given my daily experience of them), and I give thanks for this. What I cannot conclude is that children qua children are any more 'spiritual' than people at any other stage of life. And the best of their 'theology' (see, for example, Hample and Marshall's *Children's Letters to God*, 1991) seems to me to be in their questions, playful and serious, and in them being children, unconscious of any spiritual or theological quality or intention.

Church, sacraments and households

All through the journey I have been active in Christian life and worship in many varied settings around the world, including seminaries, churches, residential Christian communities and, of course, my own home, Mill Grove, and the local churches where I minister. Slowly and sometimes unexpectedly I began to find my work in Child Theology affecting more and more areas of my life and work. In such a short piece I can only hint at this process by giving one or two examples.

The sacraments (notably Baptism and the Lord's Supper) are universally understood and defined by how they relate to children, and how children relate to them. Implicit and explicit in doctrine and practice are assumptions about human sin, levels of understanding and maturity (adulthood). There is much written about these matters, and so it is not the purpose of this chapter to duplicate this thinking. Spending most of the period working on the book *Entry Point* (Willmer and White 2013) and trying to imagine myself into the story so that I could see and understand Jesus and the Kingdom of God with His choice of, and words about, a little child proved unsettling to the various traditions that inform and guide churches.

A moment of disclosure came when sitting as part of a circle at Mill Grove on Christmas Eve as we gathered to worship, pray and share Communion. I asked Michael, a young black South African, to take, break and share the bread with the person next to him. His eyes and body language conveyed total incredulity and surprise. He eventually accepted the invitation and began the process by which we served each other all around the room. Who was 'presiding', I wondered?

As I considered the theology of baptism I discovered, through his papers and articles, the journey that George Beasley-Murray, the renowned scholar and Baptist theologian (among others), had travelled. It became apparent to him that there is no watertight doctrine of baptism, and he had moved towards an understanding that saw children, and indeed all members of the church, as *catechumen*: that is, learners in the faith.

My personal journey has involved a continuous wrestling with the core notion of Church and what it is theologically and in practice. I was helped by the fact that during this period I worked on and was part of the team that produced a new edition of the Bible that was intended for everyone who wanted to read the Scriptures, whatever their age, understanding, background and faith tradition. One of the growing convictions was that it would be read in a range of settings: schools, households, churches, hospitals, prisons and villages around the world, sometimes by individuals and at other times by groups. I always imagined children being somewhere near the heart of this reading.

Increasingly I found myself addressing households and families rather than ministers and Christian educators. And as I did so it became clear that much of the idea and practice of 'church' revolves around the 'gathered community' (that is, weekly church meetings and services). But for the majority of children, most of their experience of Christian life and relationships is in households. I listened more carefully to what people were saying in my daily life and began to receive an often-repeated refrain or trope to the effect that Mill Grove was 'church'. This was the way it seemed to a range of different people who were part of this extended family and residential community, although it is certainly not a formal church in any way. But people were experiencing a closeness to God and His Word through everyday life and activity.

We have re-thought our mealtimes, and special annual events like birthdays and holidays as a consequence. But this 'household of faith' goes under the radar screen. Have we yet realised what went out with Family Bibles, Family Prayers and Grace before meals, I wonder? I have been taught by children and those who lived at Mill Grove as children, and this has changed my understanding of church.

Some years ago, I was told just before leading a service in a church in North London that they did not have sufficient adults to run the Sunday School or young people's activities that morning. So I had to re-think the pattern and content of the forthcoming service at the speed of light. We explored the early life of David together, including an improvised drama of his anointing by Samuel and the battle with Goliath. Afterwards one of the leaders of the church asked to talk with me, and my heart sank. I feared the worst, so you can imagine my surprise when he confided in me that until this service he had always assumed that to do any deep biblical study or theology the children needed to be absent. Now he told me, 'I realise that if we are to do deep theology children need to be present in some way.' And the implications of this for Christian parents, parenting and households are obvious: homes and families are places where deep theology occurs naturally, not least in the totally unforeseen questions and playful thoughts of children.

Children, Jesus and the Kingdom of Heaven

The book that Haddon Willmer and I wrote was commissioned way back in 2001, and so its conception, writing and publication span most of the period during which I was on this journey of discovery. I have kept the earliest outlines of the proposed content, and also the early drafts of a number of chapters. What becomes apparent from a comparison of the final text with these preliminary ideas is a steady, though far from linear or uniform, move from definitions of children, young people, changing conceptions of childhood, children's rights, the 1989 United Nations Convention on the Rights of the Child (UNCRC) (UN 1989), a theology of children/childhood and so on, towards God in Christ as the ground of our work. We never let go of our questions and understandings of child and childhood of course: the text of life was given. But irresistibly we found ourselves drawn to the actions and words of Jesus.

The more we stayed with and focused on just one incident in the ministry of Jesus as told in Matthew's Gospel, the clearer and more real the child in the story became. We realised that we couldn't know anything about this child called by Jesus to stand beside him, except that it was a little child. The child could have been known to the 12 disciples, or could have been a complete newcomer to them. But through this unknown and unknowable child we were able to bring our knowledge of particular children worldwide into the picture.

In the process this child became a 'little one' who represented not just actual children (and their real life-stories and experiences), but all people that Jesus was calling, whatever their age, status or situation. And this inevitably meant that we were being drawn into the story, into the circle of disciples ourselves, in and through the action of Jesus in calling this specific child. It is important to stress that this was not something we could resist if we were to be true to the nature and dynamics of Matthew's account of the event.

As adult followers of Jesus there was a tension between our identification with the child and our identification with the disciples. The book is in part a result of that tension. But it was creative rather than disabling, as we found that we were being drawn closer to Jesus. And that meant not just his person and his relationships with the little child and the disciples, but also his own calling and mission. His agenda began to take pre-eminence, and the narrative of Matthew's Gospel makes it clear that this agenda had everything to do with the Kingdom of Heaven (the Kingdom of God).

Like all followers of Jesus since, the disciples struggled with the nature, shape and demands of the Kingdom, and at this point in the story their particular focus was on what constituted greatness in this Kingdom. It is this specific question and context that frames this singular incident. As a response to their question we may presume that Jesus had many possible lines that he could have pursued. He might have told a parable, drawn from the Scriptures, or even performed a miraculous sign. Instead he called a little child and with the child standing in the middle of the group spoke thus: 'Unless you change and become humble like little children, you will never enter the Kingdom of Heaven. Therefore, whoever humbles himself (takes the lowly position of) this child is the greatest in the Kingdom of Heaven. And whoever receives/welcomes a little child like this in my name receives/welcomes me.'

The imperative for any follower of Jesus is plain for all to see. And so it was that the two of us tried to understand how it was that we should change by becoming humble. To consider ourselves otherwise outside the Kingdom was almost unbearable. The journey was a long, tortuous and surprising one, but slowly some very good news began to dawn: the process was not about spiritual discipline, study or devotion (laudable and helpful though they undoubtedly are), but at its heart had the welcome of a single little child. In the process of this single and simple action everything was crystallised. It was essential for us to stoop until we were at the child's level, and to change/adapt heart, mind and patterns of life so that this child was genuinely, fully and warmly welcomed.

It is about a real adult follower of Jesus welcoming a real child. But in the process something else was going on. Quietly, unobtrusively, there was another movement, another welcome. Jesus was being welcomed, too, and though this is almost unthinkable and indescribable, it obviously means that in some way we have become part of the story thanks to his initiative, revelation and grace in the life and work of the Kingdom of God.

Conclusion

The book, *Entry Point*, marks pretty much where I am in this journey of discovery, but I know that it does not mark the end of the journey! This short summary is intended to encourage other followers of Jesus who are privileged to be alongside children in his name to share their stories or logs of what they have encountered and discovered along the way. My journey has been possible, and hugely enriched, because it has been undertaken with many other dear friends and fellow travellers. Perhaps that is a good way of describing what the Child Theology Movement has been about thus far. Be that as it may, the journey has been an unimaginable process and blessing, full of counter-intuitive discoveries. It continues among children, and in the name of Jesus, with the general movement being towards ground level, or if you prefer, with repeated returns to the beginning, and the sense that I may be beginning to know 'the place for the first time'. It feels rather like being in a Reception class at school.

QUESTIONS FOR REFLECTION AND DISCUSSION

- What encounters with God in Christ through the Scriptures have affected and shaped your own beliefs and practices?

- What are the challenges of Loder's revised model of child development to your own assumptions and working practice, whether as a parent or children's worker?

- What are the things that you and your organisation need to let go of in order to serve God's mission more faithfully, and what are the things that you need to grasp and hold on to in his strength?

- How might you develop an understanding of God's Spirit through the spirit of children, and how better understand humankind through focusing on God, Father, Son and Holy Spirit?

- What experiences have you had in worship and sacraments, in churches and households, that have enriched your own understanding of the purpose and nature of Christian community?

References and further reading

Bunge, M. (ed.) (2001) *The Child in Christian Thought.* Grand Rapids, MI: Eerdmans.

Bunge, M. (ed.) (2008) *The Child in the Bible.* Grand Rapids, MI: Eerdmans.

Ennew, J. and Stephenson, P. (2000) *Christian and Secular Perspectives on Child Rights and Rights-based Development.* London: Tearfund.

Fowler, J. (1981) *Stages of Faith.* New York: HarperCollins.

Hample, S. and Marshall, E. (1991) *Children's Letters to God.* New York: Workman Publishing.

Hay, D. and Nye, R. (1998) *The Spirit of the Child.* London: HarperCollins.

Loder, J.E. (1995) *The Logic of the Spirit.* San Francisco, CA: Jossey-Bass.

Prevette, W., White, K.J., Ewell, C.R.V. and Konz, D.J. (2014) *Theology, Mission and Child: Global Perspectives.* Oxford: Regnum.

UN (United Nations) (1989) *Convention on the Rights of the Child.* Available at https://downloads.unicef. org.uk/wp-content/uploads/2010/05/UNCRC_united_nations_convention_on_the_rights_ of_the_child.pdf?_ga=2.216358549.247692187.1537455708-670060270.1537455708

White, K J. (2003) 'Rediscovering Children at the Heart of Mission.' In G. Miles and J.-J. Wright (eds) *Celebrating Children* (pp.189–200). Carlisle: Paternoster.

White, K.J. (ed.) (2007) *The NIrV Bible (Narrative and Illustrated).* Grand Rapids, WI: Biblica and WTL.

White, K.J. (2008) *The Growth of Love.* Abingdon: Bible Reading Fellowship.

White, K.J. (no date) *"A Little Child Will Lead Them." Rediscovering Children at the Heart of Mission.* Available at http://www.childtheology.org/wp-content/uploads/2013/02/A-little-child-will-lead-them.pdf

Willmer, H. and White, K.J. (2013) *Entry Point: Towards Child Theology with Matthew 18.* London: WTL Publications.

Young, F. (2014) *Arthur's Call.* London: SPCK.

The Contributors

David M. Csinos is Assistant Professor of Practical Theology at the Atlantic School of Theology in Halifax, Nova Scotia, Canada. He also serves as founder and president of Faith Forward (www.faith-forward.net), an ecumenical organisation for innovation in ministry with children and young people. You can learn more about David at www.davecsinos.com

Carolyn Edwards is mum to three young adults and a lecturer at Cliff College, Derbyshire, where she runs the BA Mission and Ministry programme. She has been training children's and youth workers for nearly two decades, at Cliff and at the Oxford Institute for Children, Youth and Mission, and she worked as a Children's Evangelist for her church for many years. She also ran the Scripture Union Mission in Aylesbury, and has been a regular contributor to their Light and holiday club materials. Carolyn often speaks internationally on children's spirituality, which was the subject of her first book *Slugs and Snails and Puppy Dogs' Tails: Helping Boys Connect with God* (IVP, 2011). She is currently undertaking doctoral studies on 'children and holiness', but keeps her hand in by working with some of the 11- to 14-year-olds at her local church and running the children's work at Cliff College.

Sian Hancock has worked with children and young people in a range of contexts over the years including community groups like a pre-school, primary education where she was religious education (RE) subject leader, and her local Baptist churches. She has been a tutor at Bristol Baptist College since 2008 (linked with the Institute for Children, Youth and Mission, CYM). She works part time for the Young Victims' Service, supporting children and young people who have been affected by crime. Sian has a deep sense of calling to see children develop in their own spirituality and faith journey. She is a Godly Play guide and trainer, and loves creatively inviting children (and adults) to engage with the story of God through the Bible (see www.godlyplay.uk). She is currently engaged in empirical research for her Doctorate in Practical Theology. Her research focus is 'Let the girls speak', an ethnographic study of group work with girls aged seven to fourteen.

Isobel MacDougall began her working life as a paediatric nurse and went on to qualify as a teacher, and has taught for many years in schools, colleges and universities. Her specialist field is Early Years education, and she is particularly interested in the education of teachers and Early Years workers. Now Isobel works as a parent support worker with a local charity working with families, children and young people. Isobel has four children and enjoys being a grandparent. She is a school governor for a primary school and a trustee of a charity working with teenagers.

Barbara Meardon is a former Diocesan Adviser for Work with Children and Families and primary school teacher. She has an MA in religious education in the primary school, and has lectured on religious education on PGCE courses. She has written: *8 Journey Days* (reflective days for primary schools based on Bible journeys), *Children's Quiet Days* and *Let the Children Come* (a set of reflective stations based on the United Nations' Children's Charter). She has also edited a book of children's prayers with colleagues in the Diocese of Salisbury.

Paul Nash is Chaplaincy and Spiritual Care Team Leader at Birmingham Women and Children's Hospital, a tutor at the Midlands Institute for Children, Youth and Mission, and part of the children's ministry team at his local church. He founded and is Director of the Centre for Paediatric Spiritual Care, and jointly founded and convenes the Paediatric Chaplaincy Network. He helped establish the Centre for Chaplaincy with Children and Young People at St John's College, Nottingham. Paul has written and edited a range of books about work with children, including *Supporting Dying Children and Their Families* and *Spiritual Care with Sick Children and Young People*. Paul is an Anglican priest and a trustee of the Child Theology Movement and Birmingham YMCA.

Sally Nash is founding Director of the Midlands Institute for Children, Youth and Mission (MCYM) and was part of the team that originally established CYM (www.cym. ac.uk). She is also Associate Priest, Hodge Hill Church Birmingham and Researcher at the Centre for Paediatric Spiritual Care, Birmingham Women's and Children's Hospital. Her first experience in Christian ministry was helping to run a holiday club for children on an army base in Germany with the Church Army. She supports research and writing into paediatric chaplaincy and spiritual care as part of the Birmingham Women and Children's Hospital chaplaincy team. She has written books and articles on a wide range of topics including children's spirituality, youth ministry, reflective and collaborative ministry and shame in the Church. She is an Anglican priest and Associate Minister at Hodge Hill Church in Birmingham, and a trustee of the Child Theology Movement and Frontier Youth Trust.

Martyn Payne worked with the Bible Reading Fellowship (BRF) as part of its schools and churches ministries for 15 years. Latterly he was with BRF's Messy Church team, with a particular interest in championing intergenerational church and creative Bible storytelling. Formerly he taught languages and religious education at secondary level and then for eight years worked in churches and primary schools nationally as the Children's Education Officer for the Church Mission Society. He has written a number of books, including *Creative Ways to Tell a Bible Story*, *The Barnabas Family Bible*, *Messy Togetherness* and *Messy Parables*.

Ruth Radley is a Church Mission Society Mission Partner, seconded to Birmingham Women's and Children's Hospital chaplaincy team having lived for almost eight years in South Sudan, where she continues to visit each year to teach a diploma module on child rights, participation and protection. She has worked with children for almost 30 years, originally training as a sick children's nurse, before working for a church as the children's ministry coordinator. She is passionate about children being allowed to take their rightful place in the Church, and mission being all people everywhere in partnership with each other. She holds an MA in Mission (Children) awarded by the University of Manchester at Cliff College, and has a healthy relationship with chocolate and baking!

Sam Richards is Head of Children's and Youth Work for the United Reformed Church. She has over 25 years' experience of training Christian youth and children's workers with the Institute for Children, Youth and Mission (CYM) and Oxford Youth Works. She finds life in relationships, reading, being outdoors, chocolate, making music, laughter and the mayBe community, an emerging intergenerational church in Oxford.

Andy Robertson is a (theologically trained) freelance video game expert for national newspapers and the BBC, and runs the FamilyGamerTV YouTube channel. Working on the theory and practice of spirituality in video games in a range of contexts, he runs a subscription project that provides weekly videos on the best games and technology for youth work: www.patreon.com/taminggaming

Michael Wells is father to two and grandfather to five. Originally a primary school teacher working in both urban and rural settings, he was also a chaplain at a residential school for children and young people with additional needs, and worked as a Children's Evangelist for Scripture Union. He has lectured at Cliff College and with the Oxford Institute for Children, Youth and Mission (CYM). He has an MA in Children and Religion, and loves storytelling.

Keith J. White and his wife Ruth lead Mill Grove, a Christian residential community that has been caring for children in the East End of London UK since 1899. Keith is the founder and chair of the Child Theology Movement and a trustee of Frontier Youth Trust. He was formerly chair of Children England and a member of the Care Standards Tribunal. He has written widely on child theology and contributed monthly columns to *The Therapeutic Care Journal* since 2000. Among the books he has written or edited are *A Place for Us, In His Image, Caring for Deprived Children, Why Care?, Re-Framing Children's Services, Children and Social Exclusion, The Changing Face of Child Care, The Art of Faith, The Growth of Love, Reflections of Living with Children (Vols I and II), In the Meantime, Now and Next, Entry Point* and *The NIrV Bible (Narrative and Illustrated)*. Keith is a minister who has preached, taught and contributed to conferences and symposia on every continent. He has been an Associate Lecturer at Spurgeon's College since 1978, and is a member of the Faculty of the Asian Graduate School of Theology.

Howard Worsley is the Tutor in Mission at Trinity College in Bristol, where he is also the vice principal. He is a researcher into children's spirituality and their early perceptions, a contextual theologian, and an educationalist who publishes regularly for academic journals. In 2009 he published a book on children's insights into the Bible called *A Child Sees God*. In 2013 his book, *Two Hundred Years of Anglican Church School Education*, was published by Bloomsbury. He is currently completing two books, one on parenting, entitled *How Not to Totally Put Your Children off God (A Conversation on Christian Parenting between a Father and His Sons)* and the other on theology entitled *The Strategic Child* (a book for helping adults to re-examine faith from a child's point of view through biblical storytelling, theological insights and practical application). He has previously worked as a secondary school teacher, a Scripture Union worker, an Anglican vicar, a university teacher of theology, a director of education and as a chaplain in both the higher and further education sectors. His connecting themes are contextual theology and young people, and his interests are to do with sport (the great outdoors or rugby) and travel (preferably in remote places and by off-road motorbike or canoe).

Index

Sub-headings in *italics* indicate figures.

Adams, I. 110, 117
adults 25–8
 video games 87–8, 92–3, 96
advocacy 147, 158–9
 advocating Church? 152–4
 Ironman factor 156–8
 rights and responsibilities 149–52
 rights in a global nation 147–9
 Superman, Wonder Woman or the
  Incredible family 154–6
Aesop's Fables 84, 85
AIDS 65
Ainsworth, Mary 54
Allen, H. 136, 137, 144
'alongsiding' 112–17
Alpha 142
Anthony, M. 127, 166
Anti-Bullying Alliance 38
Antonelli, P. 109
Aquinas, Thomas 124
Augustine 125
awe and wonder 171–3
 born this way 173–4
 childhood openness 174–6
 falling leaves 177–8

Barnett, B. 112
Bateson, P. 84
Batman, D. 11
BBC 110
Beasley-Murray, George 186
Beckwith, I. 133, 144, 164, 174
Beech, V. 36
behaviour 161–2
 good fences make good
  neighbours 163–5
 setting boundaries 165–9

behaviourism 22
Bell, Rob 114
Benedictines 110
Bennett, C. 45
bereavement 36
 Stages of bereavement 35
Berryman, J.W. 77–8, 133
Bible 9, 10, 102, 105–6, 115, 144
 Acts 71, 99, 126
 Bible and children 181–3
 Chronicles 98
 Colossians 126
 Corinthians 81, 126, 128, 138
 Ephesians 10
 Esther 10
 Exodus 9, 98, 149, 151, 156
 Galatians 148
 Genesis 11, 22, 78
 grandparents 68–72
 Isaiah 79, 143, 152
 Jeremiah 10
 Job 69
 Joel 71
 John 14, 53, 111, 169, 177
 Jonah 79–80
 Joshua 151
 Kings 10, 166
 Lamentations 149
 Leviticus 98
 Luke 70, 139, 174
 Mark 10, 113, 128, 136,
  138, 169, 174–5
 Matthew 9, 10, 13, 81, 128,
  136, 138, 163, 174, 188
 Peter 128

Psalms 71, 74, 78, 113, 114,
    123, 124, 125, 137, 141,
    148, 153, 166, 172
Romans 128
Samuel 10, 69–70, 157
Timothy 10, 71, 126, 136
Zechariah 70, 71
Bible Reading Fellowship (BRF) 71
Bonhoeffer, Dietrich 111
Bonner, S. 11, 14, 16
Borgman, D. 34
boundaries 106–7
    setting boundaries 165–9
Bowlby, J. 35
Bowlby, John 45, 54
boyd, d. 56
brain function 20–2
Breathe 119
British Medical Journal 149
Bronfenbrenner, U. 26–7
Brown, F. 79
Brown, V. 38
Bulger, James 24
bullying 37–9
    anti-bullying programmes 39
    discernment 36
    forgotten parties 38
Bunge, M. 11, 182
Bury Me My Love 95
Byron, T. 90

Calvin, John 125
Campbell, R. 49
camps 119
Chapman, G.D. 49
Charter, Alan 176
Chester, T. 139, 140
Child Arrangement Orders 65
child rights 147, 158–9
    advocating Church? 152–4
    Ironman factor 156–8
    rights and responsibilities 149–52
    rights in a global nation 147–9
    Superman, Wonder Woman or the
        Incredible family 154–6
Child Theology Movement
    180–1, 189 90
    Bible and children 181–3

child development theory 183–4
children, Jesus and the Kingdom
    of Heaven 187–9
children's mission and ministry 184
children's spirituality and
    children's theology 185
Church, sacraments and
    households 186–7
childhood 23–5
Childline 19–20, 38
children 18–19, 30–1
    *Bronfenbrenner's Ecological
        Systems Theory* 27
    changing landscapes of
        childhood 23–5
    into a brave new world 28–30
    medical needs at events 104
    neuroscience 20–2
    planning a session for events 105–6
    registration at events 103–4
    theories of development 22–3
    what is a child? 19–20
    who is driving the train? 25–8
Children Can 105
children's ministry 9–11, 16–17
    Church as long-term provider 12–13
    *Metaphor-based models of
        children's ministry* 15
    underpinning principles for work with
        children in the Church 11–12
    using metaphor to inform
        and understand children's
        ministry 14–16
Children's Society, The 9, 29, 53, 111
Christakis, N. 53–4, 54–5, 57
Christianity 22, 93, 98–9,
    102, 111, 114–15
    how the Christian faith has been
        handed down 123–5
Church 11–13, 111
    intergenerational relationships
        67–8, 137–9, 144
    'Messy Church' 71, 72,
        80, 101, 142, 185
    social connections 56, 57
    working with families 72–4
Church of England 154, 167
Clark, C. 137

Clery, E. 38
clowns 76–7
    the drama of playing or
        unmasking the fool? 82–4
    truth speaking in children's
        ministry 84–5
    what does it mean to clown, fool or
        'be an idiot for Christ'? 80–2
Collier, J. 10, 146, 148, 156
communication skills 43–4
Compline 115
confidentiality 46
Cooling, T. 113
CQ Researcher 38
Crowley, K. 45
Csinos, D.M. 133, 144, 164, 174
cultural diversity 151–2

D365 115
Dahlberg, G. 24
Darby, K. 37, 48
Dark Room 95
Davies, K. 59
development 34
developmental theories 22–3
Doehring, C. 34
Domoff, S.E. 90–1
Drane, J. 36
Drane, O.M.F. 36
Dunn, J. 141
Dykstra, R.C. 80

Edwards, C. 106, 165
Edwards, M. 36, 43
Elkind, D. 79
Ennew, J. 181
Enough Project 153
Erikson, Erik 29–31
Ethical Consumer 154
Evans, S. 45
events 98–9
    al fresco events 141–2
    ecumenical events 107
    event management 103–4
    Event options for different purposes 100–1
    how are we going to get there? 102
    online resources 108
    planning a session 105–7
    volunteers 106–7

where are we now? 99
where do we want to be? 99–102

Faber, H. 82
faith 49–50, 67–8
    teaching 121–3
Faith Forward 171–2
families 66–7, 136–7
    working with families 72–4
Ferguson, C. 38
Ferguson, C.J. 90
festivals 98–9
fools 76–7
    the drama of playing or
        unmasking the fool? 82–4
    truth speaking in children's
        ministry 84–5
    what does it mean to clown, fool or
        'be an idiot for Christ'? 80–2
Forde, Nigel 167
forgiveness 50
Foucault, M. 27–8
Fowler, James 45, 53–5
Fox, M. 125
Franciscan Sisters of Christian
        Charity 110
Freire, P. 14
Freud, Sigmund 29, 30
Frontier Youth Trust 88, 93
Frost, R. 163
Fuller Youth Institute 74

gaming 56, 87–8
    becoming a gamer 92
    being present 92–3
    dangers of video games 89–91
    examples that have worked well 93–5
    online resources 96–7
    untapped potential of video games 96
    violence 90
    wellbeing 90–1
    what video games are 91–2
Gardner, Howard 45, 47, 59
Gatta, J. 117
General Data Protection Regulation 104
Gentile, D.A. 90
Gerhardt, S. 20, 21
Godly Play 80, 133, 144
Good Childhood Report 9, 29, 53, 111

Gopnik, A. 20
grandparents 64–6
    biblical perspective 68–72
    online resources 74
    research on the role of
        grandparents 66–8
    working with families 72–4
Grandparents Plus 65
Greenbelt 93, 144
grief 34–7
    bereavement 36
    children handling sorrow 36
    multiple losses 37
    sharing sadness 50
    Stages of bereavement 35
Griffiths, M. 148, 156, 158
Gross, E.F. 58
Gundry, J. 175

Hart, R. 155
Hay, D. 11, 173, 174, 177
Heim, J. 56
Hertsmere Young Researchers 109
Hilfield Youth Camp, Dorset 119
Home for Good 153, 154, 176
hoodies 109–10
hospital care 40, 45, 48
Hull, John 130–4
humour 76–8
    perspectives on fun, humour
        and playing the clown 78

identity formation 57–8
    social media 58–60
Incredibles, The 155
intergenerational relationships
        56, 62, 136–9, 145–6
    al fresco events 141–2
    biblical perspective 68–72
    eating and drinking 139–40
    heavenly banquet 144
    role of grandparents 66–8
    space for play and storytelling 142–4
interventions 46
Iona 114
Islam 123

Jebb, Eglantyne 147–8
Jenkinson, S. 78
Jenks, C. 24

Jersak, B. 157
jesters 76–7
    truth speaking in children's
        ministry 84–5
Jesus 9, 10, 12–14, 68, 70, 71, 81, 82,
        99, 102, 111, 113, 115, 124–5,
        136, 138–40, 143, 147, 148,
        157–8, 163, 164, 167, 169, 172–8
    children, Jesus and the Kingdom
        of Heaven 187–9
Johnson, D. 90
Johnson, M. 14
Jones, Alistair 88, 93
Jones, Mrs 121–2, 129–34
Joseph Rowntree Foundation 29
Journey 95
Joust Mania 94
Judaism 123–4

Keenan, T. 45
Kohlberg, Lawrence 45
Koshuharov, V. 10, 11, 12, 13
Kübler-Ross, E, 35
Kuhl, A. 20

Labour Behind the Label 154
Lakoff, G. 14
Lambert, S. 110
Lausanne Forum 99
Layard, R. 141
LeFever, M. 106
Lessof, C. 29
Lindon, J. 39
Lindstrom, M. 111
liturgy 113, 115
Long Lost Families 67
loss 34–7
    bereavement 36
    children handling sorrow 36
    multiple losses 37
    sharing sadness 50
    Stages of bereavement 35
Lost Weekend 93
Loyola Press 115
Luther, Martin 125

Marano, H. 60
Marshall, K. 148–9, 152
Martin, P. 84
Masson, J. 41

May, Scottie 14, 166
Mayor, S. 149
Mbiti, J.S. 148
McCarthy, D. 110
McConnell, D. 155
meals 139–40, 143
meditation 114–15
Meltzoff, A. 20
'Messy Church' 71, 72, 80,
    101, 142, 185
Miles, G. 156
Millar, Sandra 115, 116
Miller, L. 10, 11
Mindful Christian 115
mindfulness 114–15
Minecraft® 56
modelling 115
Monastery, The 110
monastic tradition 109–10
    monks and nuns 110–11
Montgomery, H. 24, 25, 28
Moore, C. 55
Moore, L. 101
Morreal, J. 77
Moses 9, 69, 149
Moss, P. 24
Mother Teresa 51
Mott, D.W. 11
music 113, 114
Myers, B. 155
Myers-Briggs, Isabel 45

Nash, P. 37, 48
Nash, S. 37, 48
neuroscience 20–2, 110
    impact of screen time 56–7
NOOMA films 114
NSPCC 38, 106–7
Nye, R. 11, 127, 133, 173, 174, 177

O'Connell, D. 48
Ofcom 54, 60
Ogden, C. 60
online connection 54, 56–7
Open Cloister 119
Oredein, T. 109
Oxford VIVA Doorsteps 154

Palmer, S. 111
parents 61–2, 156

Parker, E. 50
Parkes, C.M. 35
Parvis, B. 148–9, 152
Pascal, B. 125
Passage 94
pastoral care 41
    assessment and care plans 45
    avoiding assumptions 43
    confidentiality 46
    duty of care and helping
       build resilience 42
    improving communication and
       making connections 43–4
    interventions 46
    name and celebrate assets 47
    parental permission 43, 46
    pastoral care with integrity 42–3
    play 48
    preparatory work 45
    providing a safe place 41
    referrals 43
    spiritual intelligence 47–8
    support for care teams 48
Pattaya Scale 99
PCN 36
Pea, R. 58
Pearmain, R. 41
Pemberton. D.K. 12
Pence, A. 24
Phillips, Zara 109–10
Piaget, Jean 22, 30, 45
pilgrimage 110–11, 116–17
play 48, 60, 65
    intergenerational relationships 142–4
    what is happening when
       children play? 79–80
    what is play? 78–9
    what types of play do we see in
       children's ministry? 80
Postman, N. 23
Powell, K. 137, 156–7
power 27–8
Powerpack 105
prayer 113, 114, 115
presence 50–1
    connected presence 61
Protestants 125
Proteus 94
Pryzbylski, A. 89

Quakers 123
quietness 113–14

Rahner, K. 125, 175–6
Rantzen, Esther 19–20
referrals 43
reflective storytelling 113–14
Reformers 125
refugees 25, 149, 151–2, 153
residential courses 119
resilience 42
retreats 115–16
Richards, A. 138
righteous indignation 50
Roberts, R. 21
Robinson, M. 21
Roehlkepartain, E.C. 12
Rogers, C. 49
Roman Catholics 115, 125, 175
Ross, C. 136, 137, 144
Runcorn, D. 111, 112–13

safeguarding 40–1
    providing a safe place 41
Safer Children in a Digital World 90
Scott, D. 147, 148
screen time 60, 87
    media addiction 89–90
    neuroscience 56–7
Scripture Union 107, 138–9
self-care 48
Shapiro, J. 87
Sharkey, P. 130
silence 113–14
Simpson, R. 110
Sinetar, M. 47
social connections 53–4
    actions for helping children form
        healthy social connections 61–2
    connected presence 61
    identity formation 57–8
    importance 54–6
    media-multitasking 58–60
    neuroscience 56–7
    play 60
    screen time 60, 87
social media 54
    identity formation 58–60
Space Team 94–5
spirituality 54, 117–19
    camps and residentials 119

children and young people
    now 111–12
    resources for spiritual
        practices 118–19
    spiritual intelligence 47–8
    spiritual practices 112–17
    spirituality in contemporary
        culture 112
Stephenson, P. 147, 181
Sticky Faith 74, 137
Stop the Traffik 154
storytelling 113–14
    intergenerational relationships 142–4
Sufis 123
Sunday School 80, 129
Sutton-Smith, B. 77
Swinton, J. 10

Taber, C. 148
Taizé 114
Taylor, C. 79
teaching 121, 133–4
    balanced pedagogy 121–3
    comparative approaches 126–8
    Comparison between connatural learning
        and systemic teaching 127
    how the Christian faith has been
        handed down 123–4
    my favourite teacher puts it
        into practice 129–33
    theological reflection on balancing
        pedagogies 124–5
Tearfund 155, 181
That Dragon, Cancer 95
theology 48, 53
    faith 49–50
    forgiveness 50
    presence 50–1
    righteous indignation 50
    sharing sadness 50
    theological reflection on balancing
        pedagogies 124–5
    unconditional love 49
theory of mind 57
Titman, P. 36, 43
transitions 39–40
truth speaking 84–5
Turkle, S. 59, 61

UN (United Nations) 25,
    28, 29, 148, 188

unconditional love 49
UNICEF 9
United Nations Convention on the
    Rights of the Child (UNCRC)
    28, 148, 156, 188
URC Charter for Children in
    the Church 137–8

van Manen, M. 130
Vygotsky, V.W. 22–3, 26, 31, 45

Wainwright, M. 32
Walker, P. 32
Wall, J. 147
Waller, T. 20
Wangerin, Walter 144
Ward, P. 99
Watkins, S.C. 61
Weinstein, N. 89
Wells, K. 148
Westerhoff, John 9, 45, 54,
    111, 112, 117, 127
White, K.J. 13, 51, 163, 164, 182, 187
Who Do You Think You Are? 67
Willmer, H. 186, 187

Wilson, L.L. 11
Wilson, R. 35
Working Families 64
working with children 33, 51
    bullying 37–9
    contexts 33–4
    loss and grief 34–7
    pastoral care and support 41–8
    safeguarding 40–1
    theological basis and rationale
        for care 48–51
    transitions 39–40
    what might be going on 34
World Health Organization (WHO) 90
Worsley, H.J. 125, 126, 129, 130
Worth Abbey, Sussex 110, 119
Wright, N.T. 116

Xcite 107

Yaconelli, M. 171–2, 178
Young Meditators 119

Zeedyk, S. 21
Zuckerberg, Mark 110